An Inspirational Book for a

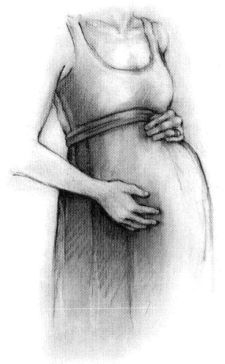

MOTHER *with* CHILD

Spiritual Enrichment
During Pregnancy

Based on the average gestation period
of 40 weeks or 280 days of pregnancy

ANNETTE MARIAN

WESTBOW
PRESS®
A DIVISION OF THOMAS NELSON
& ZONDERVAN

"Scripture taken from the NEW AMERICAN STANDARD BIBLE ®, © Copyright The Lockman Foundation 1960, 1962, 1963, 1968, 1971, 1972, 1973, 1975, 1977. Used by permission."

Excerpts from the *Catechism of the Catholic Church*, second edition, © 2000 by Libreria Editrice Vaticana-United States Conference of Catholic Bishops, Washington, D.C. All rights reserved.

Edited by: Father John Henry Hanson, O. Praem.
Norbertine Fathers of St Michael's Abbey, Silverado, Ca

Illustrated by: Lila Blakeslee, Vero Beach, FL

WestBow Press books may be ordered through booksellers or by contacting:

WestBow Press
A Division of Thomas Nelson & Zondervan
1663 Liberty Drive
Bloomington, IN 47403
www.westbowpress.com
1 (866) 928-1240

ISBN: 978-1-4908-8068-6 (sc)
ISBN: 978-1-4908-8069-3 (e)

Library of Congress Control Number: 2015907661

Print information available on the last page.

WestBow Press rev. date: 8/12/2015

This book is dedicated with love and gratitude to
OUR
MOTHER MARY

The only woman blessed by God to be *"full of grace"*.
She is the perfect source of inspiration as a mother and
as a faithful *"handmaid";* she is always at the service of
Our Lord, Jesus - for the good of all humanity.
In humble gratitude, Annette Marian

"Thus you will know them by their fruits." Matthew 7:20
We praise the Fruit of her womb!

*"This unique and inspirational book provides Scriptural
encouragement to mothers during their nine months of pregnancy.
At a time when a woman really needs encouragement,
the 'Mother with Child' book provides unparalleled support.
This perfect gift for an expectant mother cannot be
highly recommended enough."*

Steve Wood, President
Family Life Center International
Host of EWTN's Carpenter's Shop

Introduction

*I was inspired to encourage and speak up for **All Souls**:
the Mother's, Father's, and their Offspring's. I am devoted
to God's love for all parents and their children: baby
embryos, baby fetuses, babies, bambinos, bebés; all those
precious souls awaiting their entrance into the light.*
**Therefore, this book is written for all parents
and babies, no matter what
the circumstances were when the Baby was conceived.**

I write to:

1. ***Parents who are blessed under the Sacrament of Marriage*** *- Both
   the mother & father are looking forward to their child's birth with
   great joy and hope. There is a sense of security and protection in
   their union. There is an excitement to prepare a room with all the
   necessary essentials for this new family member. Yes, there could
   be some struggles in their marriage, but love moves them forward
   to overcome their problems with forgiveness, perseverance, and
   more love. They choose to turn to God and keep hope in their
   hearts.*

2. ***Parents who are not married.*** *The mother and father may marry
   in the future, or they may find that there was no true love in the
   union. Generally this union causes great pain & suffering. It is
   then the woman who will usually carry most, if not all, of the
   responsibility. The decisions will fall on her shoulders "to carry"
   through and to make the "important" and "tough choices". She
   may feel abandoned and alone in this extreme pain. Many times
   she will be coerced to abort the baby.*

*Remember: God is there for you in your time of need. He will help you!
He cares about YOU & the little one you carry. Both of you are precious
in His eyes. Your baby is not a mistake! Please know that God creates all
life. We are ALL made in His image. God gives to each & every person
the incredible gift of a SOUL, from the very moment of conception.
In All Pregnancies - God cooperates with the parents to
bring a beautiful life, body & soul – into BEING. Therefore,
all souls are made by Our Creator; **They are HIS**!*

***Their souls are so important to Him, that He gave His only Son's Life
to redeem them. So their souls are priceless! All God asks of us,
is that we make all our decisions - in and through His love.***
*We were made for this love; say yes to God's love and to life.
If you aren't feeling love and are lost in despair, hurt, fear, or your needs
(to earn, to complete school - to finish your plans) – please stop! Go to
God and find peace, love, and forgiveness. He is a Loving, Noble, and a
Merciful Creator;* ***He is the God of Second Chances.***
*Please KNOW that there are many Pro-Life groups out there that are
ready to help you and your baby in your
difficult circumstances and needs.*

*Ask God for the courage and the strength to
carry through with this great gift.*
You are called to Motherhood!
If a life has blessed your path, then God will carry you through!
*Isn't God the One who develops the child in your womb? A baby is
not just Biology 101. Are you really the one forming this little person
– giving it a brain, organs, and a SOUL? It is God who is unfolding
this cherished life in you; a life that starts at this size: "**.** " - Yes, at
the size of a period. Could you have started all life in that tiny spot,
with all it would need for all eternity? Only God is capable of that
miracle! Can parents really take credit for the DNA, brain, internal
organs, the bone structure, etc. that is forming in your womb?
Of course not! God knits the body in the womb.*
***Since it is God who is working in your womb to form an incredible life,
why should we fear this great GIFT that is unfolding?***
We all started this way!

***"For You formed my inward parts;
You wove me in my mother's womb."*** *Psalm 139:13*

Another point: God sent His Son to us for a three year Mission, to teach us how to live and literally to save us - to redeem our souls. *If it was just a three year mission, then why didn't Jesus just come as a man?* **He came as a fetus to sanctify every step of our formation & development.** *God's Plan,* which depicts incredible wisdom, has sanctified the gestation process and the womb! This fact completes God's Word: that *we truly are made in His Image.* God set this "gestation pattern" for our development. And even His Son, Jesus (who is 100% Divine & 100% human) began life in and through God's gestational design. Jesus developed each day, each week, & each month – in a woman's womb - through the nine months of gestation. *This is a powerful teaching from God - on our worth & His great care for us. Therefore, we are following God's perfect design when we nurture our offspring in the womb. The Mother of God nurtured Jesus in her womb!*

"I will give thanks to You, for I am fearfully and wonderfully made; Wonderful are Your works, And my soul knows it very well." *Psalm 139:14*

YOU & your Baby are worth everything to Our Lord! **A life is a life,** no matter how small – *the soul is still there!* **Our formation & development is God's perfect design; It reflects Jesus being formed in His Mother's womb.**

Jesus was that small in His mother's womb! Jesus was a Baby Embryo! Jesus was a Baby Fetus!

A Baby with or without a father - still has a soul! A baby with or without its mother's consent - still has a soul!

Humans do not make a soul. Our souls have a divine origin. Our souls are our eternal & direct connection to our Creator.

Look at the incredible detail and perfection in which God designs us:

Strands of Laminins

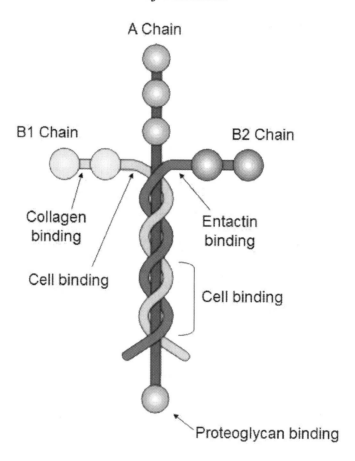

A Chain

B1 Chain

B2 Chain

Collagen binding

Entactin binding

Cell binding

Cell binding

Proteoglycan binding

Our Lord's Mark

Even at the cellular level of our body, we can see God's imprint.
Laminin, a glycoprotein, is part of our connective tissue that promotes
cellular adhesion. This protein, which holds us together, has
a molecular structure that resembles a cross!

We are wonderfully made by Our Creator & He has left His mark
within our body and soul! We are made in His image!

"He (Jesus) is the image of the invisible God, the firstborn of all creation.
For by Him all things were created, both in the heavens and on earth,
visible and invisible, whether thrones or dominions
or rulers or authorities -all things have been created
through Him and for Him. He is before
*all things, and **in Him all things hold together**." Colossians 1:15-17*

Jesus is present in our lives:
He works through us, is with us, and is in us!
Look about at His majesty – created for you. Look within at how
He builds you & upholds you in His perfect design.
"Brothers and sisters: I kneel before the Father,
from whom every family in heaven and on earth is named,
that He may grant you in accord with the riches of His glory
to be strengthened with power through His Spirit in the inner self,
and that Christ may dwell in your hearts through faith;
that you, rooted and grounded in love, may have strength to comprehend
with all the holy ones what is the breadth and length and height and depth,
and to know the love of Christ that surpasses knowledge,
so that you may be filled with all the fullness of God." Ephesians 3:14-19

Build each other UP!
Pray for each other and have confidence in God!
He will provide; He will bless You and your Little One
with incredible Joy!

*"When he falls, he will not be hurled headlong,
because the L*ORD* is the One who holds his hand.
I have been young and now I am old,
yet I have not seen the righteous forsaken or his descendants
begging bread. All day long he is gracious and lends,
and his descendants are a blessing." Psalm 37:24-26*

This book contains the Scriptures Our Lord gave me when
I had difficult pregnancies. God was there for me. He pulled me up
through the hurt & despair that were engulfing me. God gave His all,
even though I didn't truly understand the truth then; He still chose to
sustain me. He still chose to love me – even though I nailed Our Creator,
Our Lord of Life, to the Cross with my sins!

*"I would have despaired unless I had believed
that I would see the goodness of the L*ORD* in the land of the living.
Wait for the L*ORD*; be strong and let your heart take courage;
Yes, wait for the L*ORD*", Psalm 27:13-14.*

Our Lord's humility & noble Heart overwhelmed me.
So I said YES to His inspiration and Holy Will,
and He rescued both of us - my child & myself.
Our Lord loves all of us and is there for all of us.
Trust HIM - He is True!

A Loving Message from Your Little One:

I Am Here
Mom & Dad

I am in the Protective Place God placed me.
I can't wait to be held & loved by both of you.

"Make room for me that I may live." Isaiah 49:20
*"Each of us is the result of a thought of God. Each of us is willed.
Each of us is loved. Each of us is necessary." Pope Benedict XVI*

*Each Little One is a unique and precious inspiration of God's love
that has taken form in flesh - with a soul – perfectly formed by God.
That soul is the mark of the Creator and our connection to the
Blessed Trinity. **Your Baby is not just a Gift to hold & nurture;
this Little One belongs to God, and holds the spark of God within.***

*Your Child has a soul that will live forever,
an eternal connection with God!
Therefore, this book is written to inspire Parents to grow in all virtues,
that they may be encouraged and strengthened to walk in grace
so as to impart these great treasures to their children;
that each generation may grow deeper in love, faith, and hope.
God has the perfect solution to build us up -
**to make us the person
Our Lord always intended each one of us to be.***
*His Holy Scriptures are designed to inspire us; to give us hope & joy!
His Holy Scriptures are His love story to us!*

**"The word of God is alive and active, sharper than any two-edged
sword; it penetrates even to dividing soul and spirit."** *Hebrews 4:12*

*Let Our Lord speak to your heart through
His Word, as He builds you UP –
in what you need: Trust, Faith, Love, Hope, Courage, Understanding,
Wonder & Awe of God, Peace, Patience, Perseverance,
Joyfulness, Fortitude, and so much more.*

"Jesus makes all things new," *Rev. 21:5.*

*"The dignity of man rests above all on the fact that
he is called to communion with God.
This invitation to converse with God is addressed to man
As soon as he comes into being.*
*For if man exists it is because God has created him through love,
and through love continues to hold him in existence.
He cannot live fully according to truth unless he freely
Acknowledges that love and entrusts himself to his Creator."
Vatican Council II, GS 19 § 1*

*"God loves each of us
as if there were only one of us."
Saint Augustine*

"It is God who gives life. Let us respect and love human life, especially vulnerable life in a mother's womb.
All life has inestimable value even the weakest and most vulnerable, the sick, the old, the unborn and the poor, are masterpieces of God's creation, made in His own image, destined to live forever, and deserving of the utmost reverence and respect."

"All of us must care for life, cherish life, with tenderness, warmth...to give life is to open our heart, and to care for life is to give of oneself in tenderness and warmth for others, to have concern in our heart for others. We must care for life from the beginning to the end. What a simple thing, what a beautiful thing... So, go forth and don't be discouraged.
Care for life. It's worth it."

Pope Francis

Catechism of the Catholic Church, CCC

"The *unity of soul and body is so profound* that one has to consider the soul to be the "form" of the body: i.e., it is because of its spiritual soul that the body made of matter becomes a living, human body; spirit and matter, in man, *are not two natures united*, but rather their union *forms a single nature*." CCC 365

"The Church teaches that every spiritual soul
is created immediately by God –
It is not "produced" by the parents
and also that *it is immortal*: it does not perish when
it separates from the body at death, and it will be reunited
with the body at the final Resurrection." CCC 366

Mother with Child
Spiritual Enrichment during your Pregnancy

This book contains a daily Scriptural verse and an inspirational message for the average 40 weeks or 280 days of gestation.

In addition, there is a brief description of the baby's development at the beginning of each of the nine months of pregnancy.

Parents, we too must be open to grow as we care for the life God has entrusted to us. Through Holy Scripture, Our Lord directs each of us to grow in the virtues and graces He has chosen to give us, for the benefit of the whole family.

Your words, Lord, are Spirit and life.

God bless your Family!
Annette Marian

Contents

Conception

*Sperm joins with the egg to form one cell. This new life inherits
23 chromosomes from each parent - 46 total (each one being unique
& unrepeatable). This zygote, a one-celled embryo, contains all
the genetic information necessary for human development.
Nothing will be added to this remarkable human being
during gestation - except for nourishment.*

During the First Month
(1-4 weeks)

*For the next four weeks the embryo will develop rapidly. From one
cell to millions of cells, your baby will have grown 10,000 times over,
until he or she is over 1.5 in. long. The brain, spinal cord, nervous
system, and digestive tract will be established. By three weeks
the heart will start beating. Then arms, legs, muscles,
eyes and ears will begin to form.*

Day 1

**"Before I formed you in the womb I knew you,
before you were born I consecrated you."** *Jeremiah 1:5a*

*Thank you, Lord, for loving us so much that You held us dear in
your heart even before we were conceived. I know you have a
special purpose for my life & for the new life in my womb.*

From the moment of conception, 46 chromosomes with 30,000 genes
combined to determine all of your baby's physical characteristics:
his or her sex, facial features, body type, and even the color of
hair, eyes, and skin. Even more amazing, his or her intelligence
and personality - the way he or she thinks and feels; his or her
talents, tastes, athletic abilities and more – were already in place
within this genetic code. At the moment of conception, your baby
was already essentially and uniquely 'his or her own person' –
Although no bigger than a grain of sugar.
**Each and every person has their own unique identity and a soul,
coming from the mind of God – even before being formed in the womb!**

Day 2

**"For You formed my inward parts; You wove me in my
mother's womb. I will give thanks to You, for I am fearfully
and wonderfully made. Wonderful are Your works,
and my soul knows it very well."** *Psalm 139:13-14*

We are God's workmanship!
*Each one of us is a unique and special creation which God
has specifically called into being (body & soul). Therefore, we
should never lack confidence since we are children of THE
ALMIGHTY, whose great love for us gives us our dignity!*

Between 12 and 30 hours after fertilization, cell division begins. At this
stage, the cells are no larger than the head of a pin. Cells continue to divide
every 12 to 15 hours - two into four, four into eight and so on. By the time
your baby is born - 41 of those doublings will have already taken place.

Day 3

"Every good thing bestowed and every perfect gift is from above,
coming down from the Father of light,
With whom there is no variation or shifting shadow.
In the exercise of His will, He brought us forth
By the word of truth, so that we would be, as it were,
The first fruits among His creatures." James 1: 17-18

Life is a gift from God!

By His will, He has blessed us Above All other creatures in His Kingdom,
For we have been created in the image and likeness of God.
God has given us an everlasting soul. What an honor!

"Worthy are You, our Lord and our God, to receive glory and
honor and power; for You created all things, and because of
Your will they existed, and were created." Revelation 4:11

Day 4

"Your eyes have seen my unformed body and soul;
And in Your book were all written
The days that were ordained for me,
When as yet there was not one of them." Psalm 139:16

God created our unformed body & soul in love & joy! Our days were
already ordained by Him! We should not try to change what God has
intended for the great soul we carry. We should respect, honor, and
look forward to the unfolding of His Divine Plan.
What could be better than the ideal God has ordained & planned
for our Little One – who is also God's adopted child!

Thank you Lord for all the hope and dreams You have for both my life
& for the precious baby I carry. I greatly appreciate the wonderful
gifts and attributes You have already bestowed upon the baby,
through Your generous love & grace.

Day 5

**"The Spirit of God has made me,
and the breath of the Almighty gives me life."** *Job 33:4*

*Thank you, Lord, for giving me the opportunity
To live, love, and grow with my little one.
Please send Your Holy Spirit to guide me and bless me
with Your wisdom, understanding, and fortitude.
Grant that I may grow in the*
Knowledge of Your ways,
*So that I may give my very best
To You and our family.*

Biogenetics confirm that all genetic elements that mark a future person are already present from the moment of conception. This affirms Scripture – that our personhood is present before birth! Your life and your baby's life are covered by God's holy wisdom.

Day 6

"'For I know the plans that I have for you,' declares the LORD, 'plans for welfare and not for calamity to give you a future and a hope.'" *Jeremiah 29:11*

*God wants you & your baby to have a fulfilling life.
His plans are to bless your lives with His love and grace.
Pray constantly that you may stay in step
With the purpose He has designed for each of you.*

"I pray that the eyes of your heart may be enlightened, so that you will know what is the hope of His calling, what are the riches of the glory of His inheritance in the saints." *Ephesians 1:18*

Day 7

"They should seek God, that they might grope for Him and find Him, for He is not far from each one of us; for in Him we live and move and exist, as some of the poets have said, 'For we also are His offspring.'" Acts 17:27-28

*Just try to imagine what an incredible privilege God has
Bestowed on each of us, to refer to us as His offspring!
What an immense act of love and charity He has given us.
Lord, help me to always seek You with all my heart,
That I may be able to show my child (children)
What a noble blessing it is to
Live, move, and exist with You.*

Your baby is now a ball of several hundred cells, & this fertilized egg has burrowed into the wall of your womb to be sheltered and nourished.

Day 8

*"Like a shepherd He will tend His flock,
In His arm He will gather the lambs and carry them in His bosom;
He will gently lead those that are with young."* Isaiah 40:11

*During important changes in our lives, such as being pregnant
(or, for men, expecting a child), we generally spend more time
contemplating God. We think of our own origins, of our Creator,
and then we contemplate the state (merits & growth) of our own life.
As you do this, you may want to consider starting a new habit:
praying daily to your Heavenly Father.
Remember that you are praying for more than just one or two now.
Prayer will also direct your faith and trust in God to grow - Upwards!
Then you will see more clearly, and will truly know, that your
Heavenly Father really does lead and care for you & your little one.*

**"To live is to change,
and to reach perfection is to have changed often."**
Saint John Henry Cardinal Newman

Day 9

"Do not fear, for I am with you;
Do not anxiously look about you, for I am your God.
I will strengthen you, surely I will help you,
Surely I will uphold you with My righteous right hand." Isaiah 41:10

As your baby develops and grows, you will also be
growing into Motherhood & your husband into Fatherhood.
As you look ahead, you will ponder what the future may hold for your
child and your growing family. Your Heavenly Father knows your needs,
hopes, and concerns. Just keep seeking Him. He will strengthen you and
will provide for your family's concerns.
"I can do all things through Christ who
strengthens me." Philippians 4:13
Also pray to Saint Gerard Majella, the Patron Saint
Of Expectant Mothers! Ask him to intercede for your family!

Day 10

"Be anxious for nothing, but in everything by prayer and
supplication with thanksgiving let your requests
Be made known to God." Philippians 4:6

Thank you Lord for hearing my prayers, for sustaining
my baby and myself. You are so noble and good to us.
Please continue to guide every step I take.
I do need your help with the baby – the gift You have entrusted to me / us.
I look forward to all the blessings You have in store for us
With an Expectant Faith!

"Do you believe that I am able to do this?
It shall be done for you according to your faith."
cf. Matthew 9:28-30

Look at difficulties and trials as opportunities to
strengthen & clarify your faith!
"Ten thousand difficulties do not make one doubt."
Blessed John Henry Newman

Day 11

For the whole Law is fulfilled in one word, in the statement,
"You shall love your neighbor as yourself." *Galatians 5:14*

"Jesus tells us that we must give whatever it takes
to do good to one another.
Jesus gave up everything to do the Father's will;
to show us that we too must be willing to give up everything
to do God's will – to love one another as He loves each one of us.
That is why we too must give to each other - until it Hurts!"
Blessed Mother Teresa of Calcutta

"You know well enough that Our Lord does not look so much
at the greatness of our actions, nor even at their difficulty,
but at the love with which we do them."
Saint Therese of Lisieux

Day 12

"Oh give thanks to the Lord, call upon His name;
Make known His deeds among the peoples.
Sing to Him, sing praises to Him;
Speak of all His wonders." *Psalm 105:1-2*

Your baby is a wonderful gift of love from God!
Even if you feel overwhelmed at times,
He knows what is best for you and your little one.
He also knows how your lives will touch others.
Trust God & thank Him for His great design for your family.

"May you walk in a manner worthy of the Lord, to please Him in
all respects, bearing fruit in every good work and increasing in
the knowledge of God; strengthened with all power, according
to His glorious might, for the attaining of all steadfastness
and patience; joyously giving thanks to the Father, who has
qualified us to share in the inheritance of the saints
In His Light." Colossians 1:10-12

Day 13

**"When God created man,
He made him in the likeness of God."** *Genesis 5:1*

*"Man has been given a sublime dignity,
based on the intimate bond which
unites him to his Creator:
In man there shines forth a
reflection of God himself."
Pope Saint John Paul II*

*"Our Lord does not come down from Heaven every day to lie in
a golden ciborium. He comes to find another heaven which is
infinitely dearer to him -* **the heaven of our souls**, *created
in His Image, the living temples of the Adorable Trinity.
Saint Therese of Lisieux*

Day 14

**"It is I who made the earth, and created man upon it.
I stretched out the heavens with My hands
and I ordained all their host."** *Isaiah 45:12*

*It is our Heavenly Father who alone blesses us with every
sunrise & sunset. He made us, and our beautiful universe.
All this goodness and majesty He provides for us, in & through the great
love He has for each and every one of us. We are worth it to Him.*

*God guides His creation with love; we just need to perceive & admire all
He does for us. Though He doesn't need to create - He still chooses to do
so in and through His boundless splendor, majesty and profound charity.*

*"In everything, whether it is a thing sensed or a thing known,
God Himself is hidden within." St. Bonaventure*

*"In all created things discern the providence and wisdom of God,
and in all things give Him thanks." St. Teresa of Avila*

Day 15

"I have formed you, you are My servant,
O Israel, you will not be forgotten by Me." Isaiah 44:21b

Let God, the source and origin of life,
Hold you & your baby secure in His love.
He has loved you both since the beginning of time.
He is and always has been a faithful Father,
Proven True to His covenant with His people.

"With creation, God does not abandon his creatures to themselves.
He not only gives them being and existence, but also, and at
every moment, upholds and sustains them in being, enables
them to act and brings them to their final end. Recognizing
this utter dependence with respect to the Creator is a source
of wisdom and freedom, of joy and confidence." CCC 301
"Therefore let us draw near with confidence to the
throne of grace, so that we may receive mercy and find
grace to help in time of need." *Hebrews 4:16*

Day 16

"Rejoice always; pray without ceasing; in everything give thanks; for
this is God's will for you in Christ Jesus." *I Thessalonians 5:16-18*

In & Through Jesus, God's plan for humanity is realized.
In contemplating the great sacrifices the Most Holy Trinity made for us,
There should be no doubt that God's love & concern for us is Genuine!
Our life is obviously very important to Him. It is evident that
God has always, and will always, have our greatest good at heart.
*So, be at peace in the knowledge that you can **thank God in Advance**,*
For all the many blessings & graces He has prepared
For you and your child to journey through.

"If any of you lacks wisdom, let him ask of God, who gives to all
generously and without reproach, and it will be given to him.
*But he must **ask in faith without any doubting**, for the one who doubts*
is like the surf of the sea, driven and tossed by the wind. For that
man ought not to expect that he will receive anything from the Lord,
being a double-minded man, unstable in all his ways." James 1:5-8

Day 17

"Finally, brethren, whatever is true, whatever is honorable, whatever is right, whatever is pure, whatever is lovely, whatever is of good repute, if there is any excellence and if anything worthy of praise, Dwell on these things." Philippians 4:8

Keep your heart and mind always dwelling on God's excellence.
May God's peace, hope, and grace guide your life.
Don't allow your mind to fill up with fears, doubts or negativities.
Isn't God greater than all your worries and problems?
Choose to work through the grief, doubts or anger with Our Lord.
He has the perfect solution to resolve all your problems; He created you!
Then watch and see how your weaknesses will become your strengths.

"Consult not your fears but your hopes and your dreams. Think not about your frustrations, *but about your unfulfilled potential.* Concern yourself not with what you tried and failed in, but with what it is *still possible for you to do." Pope John XXIII*

Day 18

"So Elisha said, 'What then is to be done for her?', and Gehazi answered, 'Truly she has no son and her husband is old.' And he said, 'Call her.' When he had called her, she stood in the doorway. Then he said, 'At this season next year you will embrace a son.' And she said, 'No, my Lord, O man of God, do not lie to your maidservant.' And the woman conceived and bore a son at that season the next year, as Elisha had said to her." II Kings 4:14-17

Elisha was a great prophet of God, through whom the Holy Spirit of God worked in many wondrous ways. The above verses show us God's generosity and compassion in blessing the Shunammite woman with a child. The providential tone is also intriguing because we can plainly see that **this child's birth was foretold as a blessing, even before he began to grow in his mother's womb. Thus, God held this precious gift of life dear in His heart, even before conception!** *Since life is honored by God before conception, how can there be any doubt that life isn't sacred at the moment of conception and thereafter?*

Day 19

Women shall be preserved through the bearing of children if they continue in faith and love and sanctity with self-restraint. I Timothy 2:15

In bearing children we cooperate with our Creator,
Who through the parents, transmits His own image and likeness to the child.

From the beginning our baby receives a soul!
Our responsibility is to always seek the Lord's guidance, that we and our children may grow in faith, love, and in holiness.
May we give our very best to the next generation.
Remember, we are forming souls for eternity!

"The Church teaches that every
spiritual soul is created immediately by God –
it is not "produced" by the parents –
And also that it is immortal." CCC 366

Day 20

"Behold, children are a gift of the Lord,
The fruit of the womb is a reward.
Like arrows in the hand of a warrior,
So are the children of one's youth.
How blessed is the man whose quiver is full of them; Psalm 127:3-5a

Consider all the love you and your baby will share together in the future – a magnificent gift from the Lord – that will keep giving!
Ponder all the joy & fulfillment you will experience as a Mother, or as a Father.
Think of all the hugs & kisses your baby will give you.
Children are life's highest reward!
There are no greater treasures then the moments and the memories we share with our family.

Day 21

"By wisdom a house is built,
And by understanding it is established;
And by knowledge the rooms are filled
With all precious and pleasant riches." Proverbs 24:3-4

Parents, please seek God's will for your family;
Remember that we are responsible for the
spiritual upbringing of our children.
Ask the Holy Spirit to guide you in your daily contemplations
as you read Holy Scripture;
It is through His grace that your home will be established;
in and through God's wisdom, understanding, and knowledge.

"Sanctify yourself and you will sanctify society." St. Francis of Assisi

"When I was a child, I used to speak like a child, think like a child, reason like a child; when I became a man, I did away with childish things. For now we see in a mirror dimly, but then face to face; now I know in part, but then I will know fully just as I also have been fully known." 1 Corinthians 13:11-12

Day 22

"In all your ways acknowledge Him,
And He will make your paths straight." Proverbs 3:6

God is Alive and Present!
Look for *His presence* in your daily life.
In gratitude and true humility, we will recognize Him.
Then we will seek His wisdom & direction. For *all honor and glory*
will then be given to Our Lord, for nothing is accomplished without Him.

"May we serve God fearlessly,
in holiness and righteousness before Him all of our days." Luke 1:74b-75

"By creating the world God did not increase His own happiness,
since He was infinitely happy from all eternity, but He did manifest His glory externally by sharing His goodness. All creatures by their very existence show forth the glory of God, for all depend on God for their existence." Baltimore Catechism, No. 3a

Day 23

*"I will utter sayings of old, which we have heard
and known, that our fathers have told us.
We will not conceal them from our children,
But tell to the generation to come the praises of the L*ORD,
*Of His strength and His wondrous works
that He has done." Psalm 78:2-4*

*The best gift we can give our children is to tell them how faithful, loving,
and merciful their Heavenly Father has been and always will be. Then
show and explain 'His wondrous works' to them so they so can be in awe!
We should also bring the presence of Our Lord into our home by
praying together and by educating our children about God's Kingdom –
of His 'sayings of old'. Then the gifts of faith and hope will be
passed on from generation to generation.*

*"A good man leaves an inheritance [of moral stability & goodness] to
his children's children." Proverbs 13:22*

Day 24

*"I will declare Your strength to this generation;
Your power to all who are to come.
For Your righteousness, O God, reaches to the heavens,
You who have done great things; O God,
who is like You?" Psalm 71:18b-19*

*God is all powerful and can do all things. Never forget to tell your
children how great He is! For through His loving and generous heart, He
has blessed us with His Holy Spirit - who works in us to build us up and
to transform our weaknesses into His strength.*

*"God created man to manifest His glory in a special way. He gave man
an intellect and a will that he might know, praise, and love his Creator.
In the service of God, man finds his true happiness in this life."
Baltimore Catechism, no. 3b*

Day 25

"Come, let us worship and bow down,
Let us kneel before the LORD our Maker. For He is our God,
And we are the people of His pasture & the sheep of His hand.
Today, if you would hear His voice, Do not
harden your hearts." Psalm 95:6-8a

Listen to God's voice and let your heart lead you Home to Him.

"You are great, O Lord, and greatly to be praised. Great is your power,
and your wisdom is without measure. You yourself encourage man
to delight in your praise, for you have made us for Yourself, and
Our heart is restless until it rests in You."
Saint Augustine

"As soon as I set myself to pray, I immediately feel as if my heart has
been engulfed by the flame of a living love." St. Padre Pio

Day 26

"Love bears all things, believes all things, hopes all things,
and endures all things." I Corinthians 13:7

Our Lord patiently guides us forward. He never gives up on us. As loving
and faithful parents, we should follow Our Lord's example that our family
may grow in love and in His holy virtues. Then we can live and set
a good example for our children.

St. John Bosco believed in educating the whole person: 'body and
soul' united. He believed that Christ's love, and our faith in that love,
should pervade everything we do: our work, study & play. For him,
being a Christian was a full-time effort; not a once a week - Mass on
Sunday only experience. So, we must search and find Our Lord in
everything we do. Then Our Lord's love will lead us in all things.

Day 27

"I will go before you and make the rough places smooth." Isaiah 45:2a

"My God, I believe most firmly that You watch over all who hope in You, and that we can want for nothing when we rely upon You in all things. Therefore, I am resolved for the future to have no anxieties, and to cast all my cares upon You. People may deprive me of worldly goods and status. Sickness may take from me my strength and the means of serving You. I may even jeopardize our relationship by sin, but my trust shall never leave me. I will preserve it to the last moment of my life, and the powers of hell shall seek in vain to grab it from me. You are my Rock and my Refuge; my confidence in you fills me with hope.
For You, my Divine Protector, alone have settled me in hope. This confidence can never be in vain. No one, who has hoped in God, has ever been confounded." *St. Claude de la Colombiere*

"You are my hope; O Lord GOD,
You are my confidence from my youth." *Psalm 71:5*

Day 28

I will pour out water on the thirsty land and streams on the dry ground; I will pour out My Spirit on your offspring and My blessing on your descendants." *Isaiah 44:3*

Our Lord is Our Great Provider & Protector!
Consecrate your descendants to His Divine care.
He will honor your prayers & you will be assured of a blessed future.

"Against all human hope, God promises descendants to Abraham, as the fruit of faith and of the power of the Holy Spirit. In Abraham's progeny all the nations of the earth will be blessed. This progeny will be Christ himself, in whom the outpouring of the Holy Spirit will 'gather into one the children of God who are scattered abroad.' God commits himself by his own solemn oath to giving his beloved Son and 'the promised Holy Spirit . . . [who is] the guarantee of our inheritance until we acquire possession of it.'" CCC 706

Day 29

"The LORD bless you and keep you;
The LORD make His face shine on you,
And be gracious to you.
The LORD lift up His countenance on you,
And give you peace."
Numbers 6:24-26

Pray this beautiful prayer every day over your baby.
Yes, you should start praying over your baby now; now - at the
very beginning of his / her life. The Lord will honor your faith and
will bestow grace on your offspring. Our Lord is so generous.

"A faithful man will abound with blessings." Proverbs 28:20a

"Accustom yourself continually to make many acts of love,
for they enkindle and melt the soul." St. Teresa de Avila

Day 30

"He has blessed your sons within you." Psalm 147:13b

Since conception, your baby has been blessed with all the
necessary genetic information needed for his/her development.
God has also blessed your little one with many other gifts:
a spiritual soul, a unique personality, and
a calling distinctly his or her own. Only that person can accomplish
the calling God has designed for him or her alone.
Your Baby's calling is a promising future hope; watch and see it unfold!

"Take courage, stand up! He is calling for you." Mark 10:49

"We were all created for the same end –
God!" Balt. Catechism No.3, Les. 1

"To this end we always pray for (both of) you. We ask our God to make
you worthy of the life he has called you to live. May he fulfill by his power
all your desire for goodness to complete your work of faith." 2 Thess. 1:11

Day 31

*You are in the **First Trimester of your pregnancy**, so you may be
feeling more depleted than usual. Your body has to adjust and change
so as to care for **two now** (or more). So try to rest, and be at peace
in the knowledge that Our Lord is daily caring for both of you.
At the beginning, some women "just know" that they are pregnant -
from day one! Others will not suspect they're pregnant for another week
or two, since a woman's average cycle is 28 days. If you haven't seen
your Doctor yet – please do so. Your Doctor will prepare you both for
a healthy pregnancy by recommending prenatal vitamins with folic
acid, eating balanced meals, following proper exercises, and
will have you refrain from smoking or drinking alcohol, etc.*
Key point: Stay healthy for both of you!

Beginning of Second Month
(5-8 weeks)

Your baby is now cushioned in a fluid filled amniotic sac. His/ her liver, stomach, and kidneys will begin to function. The heart is fluttering at 140-150 beats per minute. The head appears to be large compared to the rest of the body, since the brain is growing so fast. Brain waves can now be detected by an EEG; in fact, the brain is already controlling the movement of muscles and organs. Arms and legs are beginning to form and your baby has already begun to develop reflexes, like responding to your touch. The skeletal structure will also begin to change from cartilage to bone.

By the end of the month, *facial features will be visible, including the eyes, ears, nose, lips and tongue. The eyes have a retina and lens, and buds of milk teeth have appeared. Your baby has its own blood type, distinct from yours. More than 100,000 new nerve cells are created every minute.*

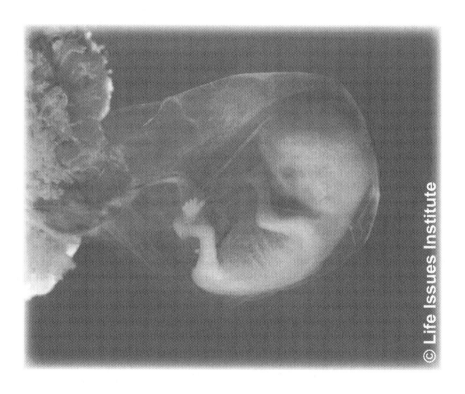

Day 32

"Just as you do not know the path of the wind and
how bones are formed in the womb of the pregnant woman,
so you do not know the activity of God who
makes all things." Ecclesiastes 11:5
We belong to God, who alone is our Creator. He always
exercises His power in wisdom and in love towards
us. He alone knows our whole being: body,
soul & spirit - from the initial moment of conception until the day He calls
us home. Our life, vocation, and children are all under God's providence
and care. God orders all, protects all, and governs all that He has made.

"The Lord beholds the ways of man and
considers every step." Proverbs 5:21

Since we do not know how to form a body, spirit, and soul in the mother's
womb, we must recognize God's omnipotence: His mastery and dominion.
This viewpoint of respecting God's authority in our life, will then help us
to form our reason and our will so as to act in God's Truth.

Day 33

"Give me now wisdom and knowledge, that I may go out and come in
before this people, for who can rule this great people of Yours?"
II Chronicles 1:10

As Solomon prayed for spiritual gifts and insight to govern
God's people, parents should also pray to the Holy Spirit to
learn how to guide their little ones.
Our children depend on us and they trust us for everything.
They look up to us and need us to direct them.
Shouldn't we also depend on Our Father and trust Him,
with the same innocence our little ones will have in us?
Who else could teach us better than our own Maker?
"The mind of the prudent acquires knowledge,
and the ear of the wise seeks knowledge." Proverbs 18:15

Day 34

*"Know that the L*ORD* Himself is God;*
It is He who has made us, and not we ourselves;
We are His people and the sheep of His pasture." Psalm 100:3

Thank you God for the gift of Motherhood.
Please help me to always give my best in caring and providing
for this child, for whom I know You have great plans. I find comfort and
assurance in knowing that we are "Your people". You will not let us go
astray for long; you rescue us when we wander into bramble bushes.
"Man is a creature composed of a body and soul, and is
made to the image and likeness of God. The soul and the body
are not loosely connected parts of man, they are united in a
substantial union to form one complete human nature. The
soul is not located in any particular member of the body but is
whole and entire in each part." Baltimore Catechism, No. 3

Day 35

"God created man in His own image, in the divine image of God
He created him; male and female He created them." Genesis 1:27

Out of noble love and with great perfection God creates us:
At the beginning of life – conception – cellular development begins. All
46 pairs of human chromosomes are present: 23 pairs from the mother
and 23 pairs from the father. A unique human life begins. Everything God
intends to give this new, little person is complete: whether it is a boy or
girl; the color of his/her hair and eyes; physical build, etc. All the genetic
makeup is present even before implantation in the mother's womb.
*Upon implantation, about **one week** later, this new life is composed of*
*hundreds of cells. By the **second week**, the new life has developed its*
*own blood cells and the baby's placenta nourishes the fetus. By the **third***
week** the baby's heartbeat and blood circulation begin. By the **fourth
***week** the brain divides into five vesicles, and this new life is ten thousand*
*times larger than it was at Day 1. By the **fifth week** brain waves are*
measurable, and the baby's eyes, legs, and hands will begin to form.
Look what God can do in Five Weeks - this is Miraculous!

Day 36

"For not one of us lives for himself, and not one dies for himself; for if we live, we live for the Lord, or if we die, we die for the Lord; therefore whether we live or die, we are the Lord's." Romans 14:7-8

Lord you have called us to go beyond our own needs and concerns. Please teach me how to share your love and compassion with others, that our family may honor your great love for us. Strengthen me that I may give my best as your daughter and as a mother (or as your son and as a father).

"Parents have the *first responsibility for the education* of their children. They bear witness to this responsibility *first by creating a home* where *tenderness, forgiveness, respect, fidelity, and service are the rule.* The home is well suited for **education in the virtues**. This requires an apprenticeship in self-denial, sound judgment, and self-mastery – the preconditions of all true freedom." CCC 2223

Day 37

My soul, wait in silence for God only,
For my hope is from Him.
He only is my rock and my salvation,
My stronghold; I shall not be shaken.
On God my salvation and my glory rest;
The rock of my strength, my refuge is in God. *Ps. 62:5-7*

Open up your heart to God. Be assured that you can put all your trust and hope in Him. He will not disappoint you! Who could be a better Guardian of your soul, or of your child's?

"Now may the God of hope fill you with all joy and peace in believing, so that you will abound in hope by the power of the Holy Spirit." *Romans 15:13*
"Who except God can give you peace? Has the world ever been able to satisfy your heart?" St. Gerard Majella

Day 38

*"Thus says the L*ORD *who made you*
and formed you from the womb, who will
help you: 'Do not fear.'" Isaiah 44:2a

God is in control! *So do not doubt. Keep hope in your heart.*
Would the Lord who formed you and your child, forget you? Hasn't
He always kept His promises to His people? The Bible depicts
many stories that show God's faithfulness and loving concern for
His people. During the Exodus, when the Hebrews were rescued
out of Egypt, there were about six hundred thousand men on
foot, not counting women and children. Other people joined them
too, along with their livestock. God cared for all of them!

"Do not fear them, for the Lord your God is
the one fighting for you." Deut. 3:22

*"***For God has not given us a spirit of timidity, but of**
power and love and discipline." *2 Timothy 1:7*

Day 39

*"***Thou will make known to me the path of life."** *Psalm 16:11a*

The Holy Spirit will counsel us in the way we should go. Seek His will
and He will lead you along a fulfilling path of spiritual growth that will
bless your life and your family's. Listen to His wisdom to prudently
discern His truth, so as not to follow the world's deceptive ideologies.

"Of all human activities, man's listening to God is the
supreme act of his reasoning and will." *Pope Paul VI*

"You have seen their abominations and their idols of ... silver and gold,
which they had with them; so that there will not be among you a man or
*woman, or family or tribe, whose heart turns away today from the L*ORD
our God, to go and serve the gods of those nations." Deuteronomy 29:17-18

Day 40

"By faith Abraham, when he was called, obeyed by going out to a place which he was to receive for an inheritance; and he went out, not knowing where he was going." Hebrews 11:8

What trust Abraham had in God's word to him! In faith and love he **obeyed God's will, without even knowing where God was taking him.** *We can't see what the future holds either, but we must trust and believe that Our Lord has prepared the best for us and our little one. Those who do not have a spouse, or perhaps do not have a job, are even more overwhelmed with uncertainties for the future. Yet God's promise to care and provide for us is still true. Trust Him and pray with a hopeful expectation. Make it a positive quest, even though you don't know all the details yet. God is always one step ahead of you, preparing the way!*

"Behold, I am going to send an angel before you to guard you along the way and to bring you into the place which I have prepared." Exodus 23:20

Day 41

"Now it shall be, if you diligently obey the Lord *your God, being careful to follow all His commandments; then blessed shall be the offspring of your body and the produce of your ground."* Deuteronomy 28:1a, 4a

The Lord emphasizes obedience to His commandments. He hopes that we will give our whole heart to Him. In doing so, He promises to richly reward us and our offspring for this love and faithfulness to Him.

"The Virgin Mary most perfectly embodies the obedience of faith.
By faith Mary welcomes the tidings and promise brought by the angel Gabriel, believing that **"with God nothing will be impossible"** and so giving her assent: "Behold I am the handmaid of the Lord; let it be [done] to me according to your word." *CCC 148*

Day 42

"I call heaven and earth to witness against you today, that I have set before you life and death, the blessing and the curse. So choose life in order that you may live, you and you descendants, by loving the LORD your God, by obeying His voice, and by holding fast to Him; for this is your life and the length of your days." Deuteronomy 30:19-20a

The CHOICE is simple: *we can live a life with God full of love and blessings* **or** *we can live a life without God. Without Him, our life spirals down into a meaningless existence full of despair. So seek the Truth and His true LOVE - that you may* **Choose Wisely for yourself and your child.** **IF** *you are still questioning whether you should have your baby, please* **don't let despair & fear push you in the wrong direction.** *Yes, the pressures and fears are overwhelming, especially if your heart was abused and broken.* **However, God is bigger than your problems & HE will HELP YOU!**

"I cannot fear a God who made himself so small for me!" St. Thérèse

Day 43

"I will bless her, and indeed I will give you a son by her. Then I will bless her, and she shall be a mother of nations; kings of peoples will come from her." Genesis 17:16

If God wills it, then it will be! Not only is God faithful to His promises, but He always carries out His purpose, even if it seems like foolishness to the world. Although Abraham and Sarah were advanced in age, God still chose to work through them as He established His everlasting covenant for all of us. God's blessing to nations was fulfilled through the birth of their son, Isaac.
Note that this child was promised before conception.
Their roles in history were prophesized and came to be as God said it would be. **Our life's impact has great meaning too,** *beyond our imagination. Many are blessed from one life.*
Many will be blessed from your life and your child's.

Day 44

"By faith even Sarah herself received the ability to conceive, even beyond the proper time of life, since she considered Him faithful who had promised. Therefore, there was born even of one man, and him as good as dead at that, as many descendants AS THE STARS OF HEAVEN IN NUMBER, AND INNUMERABLE AS THE SAND WHICH IS BY THE SEASHORE." Hebrews 11:11-12

All things are possible in and through God. None of us can fathom the mind of God, nor the depth of His admirable heart, that lovingly prepares every detail of our lives. Looking back makes it clear that generations have been born that are as 'innumerable as the sand' on the beach. Thus we cannot perceive God's infinite capacity; yet, His creation mirrors the inexhaustible love & compassionate care that depicts His True Nobility.

"The Lord declares to his people, 'I have loved you with an everlasting love; therefore I have continued my faithfulness to you.'" Jeremiah 31:3

Day 45

"By faith Moses, when he was born, was hidden for three months by his parents, because they saw he was a beautiful child; and they were not afraid of the king's edict." Hebrews 11:23

*Can you imagine having such faith, that you could send your child drifting down a river in a basket to save his life? Your infant child, who cannot swim, floats away. And what if the basket turns over? Moses' parents had great faith and courage to let go! Yet look how their trust was blessed: Moses was taken to the palace by Pharaoh's daughter; and then by the grace of God, Moses led his people out of Egypt and captivity! This is **a great example of how the sacrifices we make in faith - will bring incredible blessings! Listen to God's direction in your life! "If God is for us, who can be against us?" Romans 8:31***

Day 46

"He has remembered His covenant forever, the word which
He commanded to a thousand generations." Psalm 105:8

God's word has been true from generation to generation, down
through the centuries. Those who have eyes to see and ears to hear
will testify that God has always been faithful! His plan is perfection.

"God calls Moses from the midst of a bush that burns without being
consumed: "I am the God of your father, the God of Abraham, the God
of Isaac, and the God of Jacob." God is the God of the fathers, the One
who had called and guided the patriarchs in their wanderings. *He is the*
faithful and compassionate God who remembers them and his promises;
He comes to free their descendants from slavery. He is the God who,
from beyond space and time, can do this and wills to do it, *the God*
who will put His almighty power to work for this plan." CCC 205

Day 47

"'If You can do anything, take pity on us and help us!'
And Jesus said to him, 'If You can?'
'All things are possible to him who believes.'
Immediately the boy's father cried out and said,
'I do believe; help my unbelief.'" Mark 9:22-24

This is an honest prayer we should all say daily, to stay humble:
"Lord I do believe; help my unbelief."

"Start by doing what is necessary, then do what is possible,
and suddenly you are doing the impossible." St. Francis of Assisi

"It is not the actual physical exertion that counts towards a
man's progress, nor the nature of the task, but the spirit of faith
with which it is undertaken." St. Francis Xavier

Day 48

**"Thou, O Lord, are a shield about me,
My glory, and the One who lifts my head."** *Psalm 3:3*

*"God protects and delivers a humble man; the humble He loves
and consoles.* **To the humble He inclines Himself and bestows**
abundant graces, raising him from abasement to glory. **To** *those
He reveals His secrets, and lovingly calls & draws them to Himself.
The humble man, though he may suffer shame and
be in the midst of trouble, will remain in great peace; for
he trusts in God, and not upon the world."* Thomas à Kempis

*"What will be the crown of those who, humble within and humiliated
without, have imitated the humility of our Savior in all its fullness."*
St. Bernadette

Day 49

**"Little children, let us not love with word or with tongue,
but in deed and truth."** *I John 3:18*

*Our Lord needs faithful laborers in His fields. As a mother or father,
you have a great opportunity to teach your child about God's truth
and all He has done for us. Then as your child matures, he/she will
carry on in your footsteps, serving the Lord with a willing heart.*
**"The proof of love is in the works. Where love exists, it works
great things. But when it ceases to act, it ceases to exist."**
Pope St. Gregory the Great

*"May the Lord, the God of your fathers, increase you
a thousand-fold more than you are and bless you, just
as He has promised you!" Deuteronomy 1:11*

Day 50

*"For we are His workmanship, created in Christ Jesus
for good works, which God prepared beforehand
so that we would walk in them." Eph 2:10*

*God has given us the gift of His Son, and through Christ, we have the
grace to walk in His light. Even if others perceive us to be failures,
Our Lord affirms us. By His grace, He can transform our human
weaknesses to accomplish good for His Kingdom. Walk with Him,
and He will teach you how to be a wonderful mother / father.*

**"There is now no condemnation for those who are in Christ Jesus.
For the law of the Spirit of life in Christ Jesus has set you free from
the law of sin and of death." Romans 8:1-2**

"We are not the sum of our weaknesses and failures; we
are the sum of the Father's love for us and our real capacity to
become the image of his Son." *Pope Saint John Paul II*

Day 51

*"And He has said to me, "My grace is sufficient for you,
for power is perfected in weakness." Most gladly, therefore,
I will rather boast about my weaknesses, so that the power
of Christ may dwell in me." 2 Corinthians 12:9*

*At times when we consider the awesome responsibilities of having a
child, we may feel overwhelmed by our fears or weaknesses. Pray to
the Lord! He will give you the grace to learn and grow with the daily
needs of motherhood. Walk step by step with Christ. If we trust God,
our weaknesses will be transformed to accomplish all through Christ.*

*"Few souls understand what God would accomplish in them if they
were to abandon themselves unreservedly to Him and if they were
to allow His grace to mold them accordingly." St. Ignatius Loyola*

Day 52

"He will call upon Me, and I will answer him;
I will be with him in trouble;
I will rescue him and honor him." Psalm 91:15

"Love consumes us only in the measure of our
self-surrender." St. Therese of Lisieux

Prayer for a Holy Motherhood
O good St. Gerard, powerful intercessor before God and
Wonder-worker of our day, confidently I call upon you to seek your
aid. On earth you always fulfilled God's design; please help me now
to do the Holy Will of God. Implore the Lord of Life, from whom all
paternity proceeds, to bless and protect my offspring that I may
raise up children to God in this life, and heirs to the
Kingdom of His glory in the world to come. Amen.

Day 53

"For He will give His angels charge concerning you,
To guard you in all your ways.
They will bear you up in their hands,
Lest you strike your foot against a stone." Psalm 91:11-12

Our Lord has set His angels to watch over you and your baby. So,
*pray to your Guardian Angel **and** to your baby's Guardian Angel.*
Isn't it amazing that right now you are doubly blessed with
TWO Guardian Angels - to look out for both of you!

The Guardian Angel Prayer
Angel of God, my guardian dear, to whom His love entrusts me here, ever
this day [night] be at my side to light and guard, to rule and guide. Amen.

Day 54

*"The L*ORD *is my strength and my shield;*
My heart trusts in Him, and I am helped;
Therefore my heart exults,
And with my song I shall thank Him." Psalm 28:7

I thank You, Lord, and I praise You, for You are my great protector
and encourager. Through your steadfast love and generous grace, my
spirit is consoled and renewed. I know You are also protecting my little
one as he/she grows. My heart is grateful for all that You are doing for us.

"In order that people might feel confidence that they can find God,
and certainly that He will not desert them afterwards, He made Himself
one of them and laid Himself in the arms of a Virgin, bound hand
and foot in swaddling bands, so that he could not flee from those
who came in quest of him." *St. John of Avila*

Day 55

*O L*ORD, *how many are your works!*
In wisdom You have made them all;
The earth is full of Your possessions.
You open your hand, they are satisfied with good. Psalm 104:24, 28

Rest assured that God cares for all of our daily needs. In wisdom the
Lord carefully created the earth to shine forth His goodness: through
our sun, the seasons, our land, water, vegetation, animals, etc. All these
incredible works are a generous gift for us given directly from His hand.
Yet God holds us dearer than all His majestic creation.

He predestined us to adoption as sons through Jesus Christ to Himself,
according to the kind intention of His will, to the praise of the glory
of His grace, which He freely bestowed on
us in the Beloved." *Ephesians 1:5-6*

Day 56

"You send forth Your Spirit, they are created;
And You renew the face of the earth." Psalm 104:30

"Our bodies are shaped to bear children, and our lives are a
working out of the processes of creation. All our ambitions
and intelligence are beside that great elemental point."
Saint Augustine

"Abandon yourself entirely into the arms of our heavenly
Father's divine goodness." St. Padre Pio

"Celebrate the feast of Christmas every day, even every moment in the
interior temple of your spirit, remaining like a baby in the bosom of
the heavenly Father, where you will be reborn each moment in the
Divine Word, Jesus Christ." St. Paul of the Cross

Day 57

"Therefore let us draw near with confidence
to the throne of grace, that we may receive mercy
and find grace to help in time of need." Hebrews 4:16

Go to your Father in confidence; He is always waiting to hear from you.
He will bless your efforts with His great love and grace.
He knows all your needs, especially now as you
carry a new life & soul within you. Trust Him;
He's there for both of you at every step.

"When you are unable to take big steps on the path that leads
to God, be content with little steps, patiently waiting until you
have the legs to run; or better still, wings to fly. Be content with
being, for now, a little bee in a hive, which will soon become
a big bee, capable of producing honey." St. Padre Pio

Day 58

"Can a woman forget her nursing child,
And have no compassion on the son of her womb?
Even if these may forget, I will not forget you.
Behold, I have inscribed you on the palms of My hands." Isaiah 49:15-16a

"What made you establish man in so great a dignity?
Certainly the incalculable love by which you have looked on
your creature in yourself! You are taken with love for her;
for by love indeed you created her,
by love you have given her a being capable
of tasting your eternal Good."
St. Catherine of Siena,
Dialogue 4, 13 "On Divine Providence"

"I will not take my love from you, nor
will I ever betray my faithfulness." Psalm 89:33

Day 59

"For those whom He foreknew, He also predestined to become
conformed to the image of His Son, so that He would be
the firstborn among many brethren." Romans 8:29

*"When **Christ became incarnate** and was made man,*
he recapitulated in himself the long history of mankind
and procured for us a 'short cut' to salvation, so that
what we had lost in Adam, that is, being made in the image
and likeness of God, we might recover in Christ Jesus.
For this reason Christ experienced all the stages of life,
thereby giving communion with God to all men."
St. Irenaeus, Adv. haeres. 3, 18

Christ became Incarnate in His Mother's womb!
To save us - The Word became flesh!

Day 60

*"Who is the man who fears the L*ORD*?*
He will instruct him in the way he should choose.
His soul will abide in prosperity,
And his descendants will inherit the land." Psalm 25:12-13

All parents hope to 'do their best' for their children. So be prepared for
your new roles as parents by first starting the habit of praying together.
Then study, read and continue praying daily, so as to cultivate a
deeper relationship with God. Then you will grow in faith to be
prepared to teach your child to know, love and serve God.
The primary role of great parents
Is to be ladders by which your children can climb to heaven.

Dear Father, grant us the Spirit of Fear (Awe) that we may be filled with
a loving reverence towards You, so as to serve You with all our hearts.

Day 61

*"The L*ORD *will accomplish what concerns me;*
*Your loving kindness, O L*ORD*, is everlasting;*
Do not forsake the works of Your hands." Psalm 138:8

The Breastplate of St. Patrick

Christ as a light,
Illumine and guide me!
Christ as a shield, overshadow and cover me!
Christ be under me! Christ be over me!
Christ be beside me, On the left hand and right!
Christ be before me, behind me, about me;
Christ this day be within and without me!

Day 62

"The free gift of God is eternal life in Christ Jesus our Lord."
Romans 6:23b

The gift of eternal life is so incredible that it is difficult to fathom what God is offering us! Stop and really focus for a moment on eternity,
forever and ever...
It's hard to comprehend this concept with our definitive view of time. When you are pregnant it is normal to look forward, (especially as the baby grows larger) to the future. The point is - we must take this message to heart. **Our perspective and goals drastically change** *when we Contemplate our lives in terms of our TRUE DESTINY.*

"We must often draw the comparison between time and eternity. This is the remedy of all our troubles. How small will the present moment appear when we enter that great ocean!" St Elizabeth Ann Seton

Day 63

The Triumph of Faith
"Now faith is the assurance of things hoped for, the conviction of things not seen."
Hebrews 11:1

We must learn to wait patiently upon our Lord's leading, as we seek a deeper inner life. Christ is always there for us. He is continually teaching us, even during those "quiet" times when we wait anxiously for an answer. It is hard to wait and persevere in blind hope, yet in time we will look back and understand God's wisdom and design —His perfect plan for our life.
Pregnancy is a lesson in hope and faith —
It is a conviction of things not fully seen. Only in time are we able to comprehend just how much our faith has grown, in and through our faithful, steadfast spirit.
Your hope and faith will give birth to great love in a few months!

Third Month
(9-13 weeks)

Your uterus will double in size, as your baby grows to be about three inches long with a weight of about an ounce. His/her muscle coordination is developing rapidly. Your baby can now turn his or her head, open and close its' mouth, and can make a tight fist. Fingerprints are evident in the skin, and fine hair has begun to grow on the head. The baby's nose, lips, eyes, eyelids, and ears are more apparent. The umbilical cord is well formed now with two arteries. One carries amniotic fluid to help develop his/her respiratory system. By the end of the month, your baby's sex may be determinable. In addition, you may be able to hear your baby's heartbeat with a Doppler ultrasound device. Your clothes may be feeling tighter now, and you may also be feeling warmer than usual. During pregnancy, you may gain a total of 20-30 lbs; most of this weight will be due to the baby, placenta, and amniotic fluid.

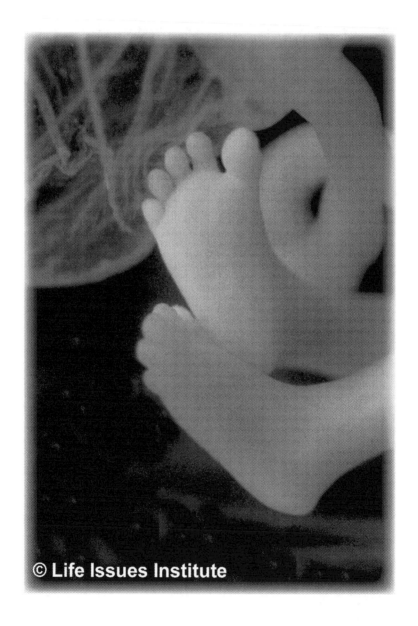

Day 64

"The angel said to her, "Do not be afraid, Mary; for you have found favor with God. And behold, you will conceive in your womb and bear a son, and you shall name Him Jesus." Luke 1:30-31

Ponder Mary's "Yes" to God's invitation to be the Mother of Jesus.
Her love of God overcame any fears or concerns for the future, since she trusted completely in His providence.
Since God carefully planned the coming of His only Son, don't you think that He must already have very noble plans for you and your little one, as adopted children of God? Would God prepare and sacrifice so much without having a very special purpose for YOU & YOUR BABY?
He will make a path for you & your family. Have confidence in Him!

"Commit your works to the LORD and your plans will be established." *Proverbs 16:3*

Day 65

"And Mary said, "Behold, the handmaid of the Lord; May it be done to me according to your word." And the angel departed from her." Luke 1:38

Mary entrusted God with her "Yes", *even though she knew her life would drastically change and be one of great sacrifices. She grew up in the Temple and studied the Holy Scriptures,* **so she knew the great price God intended to pay to redeem us.** *It was her great love and faith in God, that gave her the* **courage to follow God's will.**
Appropriately, Mary is honored and blessed above all women, throughout all generations, as the **"Mother of the Redeemer".**

"If you could have preexisted your mother, would you not have made her the most perfect woman that ever lived—one so beautiful she would have been the sweet envy of all women, and one so gentle and so merciful that all other mothers would have sought to imitate her virtues? Why, then, should we think that God would do otherwise?" - Archbishop Fulton Sheen

Day 66

The Magnificat
"Mary said: 'My soul exalts the Lord,
and my spirit has rejoiced in God my Savior.
For He has had regard for the humble state of His Handmaid;
For behold, from this time on all generations will count me blessed.
For the Mighty One has done great things for me; and holy is His name.
AND HIS MERCY IS UPON GENERATION AFTER GENERATION
TOWARD THOSE WHO FEAR HIM.'" Luke 1:46-50

Through Mary's 'Yes', God's promise to send His Son is realized.
*Mary recognizes and receives the honor God has bestowed on her with a very humble and grateful heart. She understands the magnitude and the extent of her **"Yes"** to God. We should also say **"yes" to the Lord's will** in our life, that we may be a vessel of His love & grace for others.*

"Your body is a temple of the Holy Spirit who is in you, whom you have from God, and that you are not your own?" I Cor. 6:19

Day 67

"I delight to do Your will, O my God;
Your Law is within my heart." Psalm 40:8

"The one who accepted 'Life' in the name of all and for the sake of all was Mary, the Virgin Mother; she is thus most closely and personally *associated with the Gospel of life. Mary's consent at the Annunciation and **her motherhood stand at the very beginning of the mystery of life which Christ came to bestow on humanity** (cf. Jn 10:10). Through her acceptance and loving care for the life of the Incarnate Word, human life has been rescued from condemnation of a final and eternal death. For this reason, Mary, 'like the Church of which she is the type, is a mother of all who are reborn to life. She is in fact the mother of the Life by which everyone lives, and when she brought it forth from herself she in some way brought to rebirth all those who were to live by that Life.'"*

Pope Saint John Paul II
Encyclical Evangelium Vitae,
"On the Value and Inviolability of Human Life",102

Day 68

Jesus taught us to pray this way:
"Our Father who art in heaven, hallowed be Thy name.
Thy kingdom come; Thy will be done, on earth
as it is in heaven." Matthew 6:9-10

*There are times when a pregnancy may become a crisis or a burden for a woman or a man. The woman may believe that she is too young or too old. She may be troubled with significant problems: a difficult relationship or one that wasn't true; financial stresses; educational desires; and/ or peer pressure - being misled by media, society & cultural views. The man may not understand his role as a protector and guide; he may not truly love the person he is in a relationship with; and/or he may not want to carry the responsibilities of marriage and raising a family. Yes, we do have a free will, but God's hope is that we will love and trust Him enough - **to choose His will in our life, and in turn to choose life for our offspring. Life is a very precious and sacred GIFT. We are all called into being by God. Not one of us is a mistake!***

Day 69

"Not everyone who says to Me, 'Lord, Lord,' will enter the kingdom of heaven, but he who does the will of My Father who is in heaven will enter." Matthew 7:21

*It may seem difficult at times to follow God's will. It's easy to get caught up in our own needs and desires. But as we grow and mature in our faith, we will find that a life spent on "self" is very unrewarding and very empty. **We can only find our true self - in the giving of our self.** Ask Our Lord to help you take the first step towards growing in understanding so as to follow and serve Him. He will bless your courage and reliance on Him with a steadfast spirit, and the necessary grace to persevere in His will.*

"I would have despaired unless I had believed that I would see the goodness of the LORD In the land of the living. Wait for the LORD; Be strong and let your heart take courage; Yes, wait for the LORD." Psalm 27:13-14

Day 70

In the Garden of Gethsemane, Jesus^{said,} *"Father, if You are willing, remove this cup from Me; yet not My will, but Yours be done." Luke 22:42*

Jesus is the Son of God, yet, He still chose to be obedient to the Divine Will of His Father. Jesus said YES to make the ultimate sacrifice for us, knowing what this sacrifice would entail. In doing so, Jesus accomplished His Father's will to become our Savior and our Role Model.

*God could have sent an angel to fulfill His covenant promise with man. However, He chose to send His only Son, Jesus – **as a FETUS** – to consecrate life in the womb. Therefore, Jesus was that small developing embryo and fetus at: 1-7 days, 2-7 weeks, 2-3 months, 4-6 months, and 7-9 months. Jesus spent nine months in His mother's womb, just as we did.*
Christ's Incarnation (becoming flesh) was a great Act of Humility
*By God Himself - which **established the sacredness of all life**.*
We are all made in His image from Day ONE!

Day 71

"Strength and dignity are her clothing,
And she smiles at the future." Proverbs 31:25

Description of a Worthy Woman
The Old Testament verse above is part of an oracle taught by the King's Mother to King Lemuel. It depicts a woman with outstanding qualities and virtues, who led a life centered in God.

Dear Holy Spirit please perfect in my soul the work
of Your grace and grant me:

*The **Spirit of Wisdom** that I may live towards the goal of being with You eternally, and not to live according to worldly standards;*
*The **Spirit of Understanding** to enlighten my mind with Your Truth*
& Your Holy Scripture; and
*The **Spirit of Counsel** that I may ever choose to follow your ways,*
to please You, my Lord, Amen.

Day 72

"The counsel of the LORD *stands forever,*
The plans of His heart from generation to generation. Psalm 33:11

Jesus to St. Catherine of Siena: "I distribute the virtues quite
diversely; I do not give all of them to each person, but some to one,
some to others. . . . I shall give principally charity to one; justice
to another; humility to this one, a living faith to that one. . . . And
so I have given many gifts and graces, both spiritual and temporal,
with such diversity that I have not given everything to one single
person, so that you may be constrained to practice charity towards
one another. . . . I have willed that one should need another and
that all should be my ministers in distributing the graces and gifts
they have received from me." St. Catherine of Siena, Dial. I, 7.
May we learn to live and grow according to Our Lord's counsel and
the loving intentions of His heart. Promote respect & gratitude in
your home, to every member of the family.

Day 73

"Let us show gratitude, by which we may offer to God
an acceptable service with reverence and awe." Hebrews 12:28

The Church sees in Mary the highest expression of the "feminine
genius" and she finds in her a source of constant inspiration. Mary called
herself the "handmaid of the Lord" (*Luke* 1:38). Through obedience to
the Word of God she accepted her lofty yet not easy vocation as wife
and mother in the family of Nazareth. Putting herself at God's service,
she also put herself at the service of others: ***A service of love.****
Pope Saint John Paul II, Letter to Women

"In Mary God has given back woman's lost crown. In her, the woman
has become queen. The only one purely created being who is allowed to
enter into the most intimate imaginable union with God is a woman: the
Queen of heaven and earth. In her, all the members of her sex experience
the solar radiance of feminine dignity and beauty, and a piece of their
own God-given greatness." - Fr. Joseph Kentenich, Servant of God

Day 74

"In the days of His flesh, He offered up both prayers and supplications with loud crying and tears to the One able to save Him from death, and He was heard because of His reverence. Son though He was, He learned obedience from the things which He suffered; and having been made perfect, He became the source of eternal salvation for all who obey Him." Hebrews 5:7-9

"In the Letter to the Hebrews, 'Paul emphasizes three strong words: he says that *Jesus 'learned, obeyed and suffered'*. It's the opposite of what had happened to our father *Adam, who did not want to learn* what the Lord commanded, *who did not want to suffer, or obey. Instead, even though Jesus is God, He 'is annihilated, He humbled Himself and became a servant.* This is the glory of the Cross of Jesus': Jesus came into the world to learn how to be a man, and by being a man, to walk with men. He came into the world to obey, and He obeyed. But *He learned this obedience from suffering.* Today, through this obedience, this self-abnegation, this humiliation, through Jesus, *that promise becomes hope."* Homily of Pope Francis - Sept. 15, 2014

Day 75

"We know that God causes all things to work together for good to those who love God, to those who are called according to His purpose." Romans 8:28

Sometimes our soul is disturbed when all around us everything seems to be going wrong. *Remember that God is in control.* He does work out everything for the good of our soul, in His Holy Will. Stay hopeful as *you & your baby journey 'according to His purpose'.*

Dear Holy Spirit please bless me with your Spirit of Fortitude, that I may bear my cross with You and may overcome with courage all the difficulties & temptations that oppose my salvation, Amen.

"We have obtained an inheritance, having been predestined according to His purpose who works all things after the counsel of His will." Ephesians 1:11

Day 76

**The Angel Gabriel foretold Christ's birth, and also John the Baptist's:
"And behold, even your relative Elizabeth has conceived a son in her
old age; and she who was called barren is now in her sixth
month. For nothing will be impossible with God."** *Luke1:36-37*

*Gabriel's message is proof of God's providence and of His great love for
all humanity. God's loving intent is evident in the careful planning and
preparation taken to fulfill His promise for our salvation. Scripture also
gives us an insight into Elizabeth's steadfast faith. For although she was
elderly and had been barren for many years, she still believed that God's
word would be fulfilled. Her faith was greatly rewarded, for there was
no greater* **Witness to the Light - than John the Baptist.**

**"The angel said to him, 'Do not be afraid, Zacharias, for your
petition has been heard, and your wife Elizabeth will bear you
a son, and you will give him the name John.'"** *Luke 1:13*

Day 77

**"He makes the barren woman abide in the house
As a joyful mother of children."** *Psalm 113:9*

**God said to them, "Be fruitful and multiply,
and fill the earth."** *Genesis 1:28*

*"Man and woman were made 'for each other' –
not that God left them half-made and incomplete: he created them
to be a communion of persons, in which each can be a "helpmate" to
the other, for* **they are equal as persons** *('bone of my bones. . .')
and complementary as masculine and feminine.
In marriage God unites them in such a way that, by forming
'one flesh', they can transmit human life: 'Be fruitful and multiply,
and fill the earth.' By transmitting human life to their descendants,*
**man and woman as spouses and parents cooperate in
a unique way in the Creator's work."** *CCC 372*

Day 78

An Incredible Promise:

*"I will give you a new heart and put a new spirit within you; and
I will remove the heart of stone from your flesh and give you a heart
of flesh. I will put My Spirit within you and cause you to walk in
My statutes, and you will be careful to observe
My ordinances." Ezekiel 36:26-27*

**"Do you wish to rise?
Begin by descending.
Do you plan a tower that will pierce the clouds?
Lay first the foundation of humility."** *St. Augustine*

*"Create in me a clean heart, O God,
and renew a right spirit within me." Psalm 51:10*

Day 79

**"Now at this time Mary arose and went in haste to the hill country, to a
city of Judah, and entered the house of
Zacharias and greeted Elizabeth.
When Elizabeth heard Mary's greeting, the baby leaped in her womb;
and Elizabeth was filled with the Holy Spirit. And she said, "For behold,
when the sound of your greeting reached my ears, the baby
leaped in my womb for joy."** *Luke 1:39-41, 44*
*This Scripture is Proof Positive: that an infant in the womb is blessed
by God's Holy Spirit. It is clear that the baby fetus, John the Baptist,
was inspired to know that Mary was pregnant with Our Lord. John
cannot see Jesus – they are wombs apart! Yet,* **both babies are in
the womb communicating to the world – that they are there! Baby
fetus John is announcing Jesus, as he jumps for joy.** *This is proof
that God has truly blessed the little lives we carry in our womb
with His Holy Spirit. Fetuses proclaiming the Truth - Wow!*

"They [John and Jesus] were both alive while still in the womb.
Elizabeth rejoiced as the infant leaped in her womb; Mary glorifies
the Lord because Christ within inspired her. Each mother recognizes
her child and each is known by her child who is alive, being not
merely souls but also spirits." – Tertullian, *De Anima* 26.4

Day 80

"Elizabeth cried out with a loud voice and said to Mary,
'Blessed are you among women, and blessed is the fruit of
your womb! And how has it happened to me, that the
Mother of My Lord would come to me?'" Luke 1:42-43

Baby fetus John enlightens his mother Elizabeth as he jumps for JOY
in her womb, because he KNOWS - that he is in the divine presence of
Baby Fetus Jesus – who is in the womb of His Mother Mary.
Jesus, the Lord of Life, was dependant on His Mother's love as a small
developing fetus in the womb. He was also dependant on Mary for
His life's nutrients as he grew from this size: "." to His birth
size (norm being 19-20 in). Motherhood and all of humanity have
been blessed through Mary, who welcomed His Divine Nature from
the very beginning! May the Holy Spirit inspire us to know the value
and dignity that every life warrants, starting from conception!

Day 81

"And you, child, will be called the prophet of the Most High;
For you will go on BEFORE THE LORD TO PREPARE HIS WAYS;
To give to His people the knowledge of salvation by the
forgiveness of their sins, Because of the tender
mercy of our God." Luke 1:76-78

Zacharias was enlightened by the Holy Spirit when he prophesied about
*John the Baptist's future mission. For his son was born **to be the one***
*called by God to **prepare the way for Christ**. John's mission was*
thus clearly defined in God's mind even before John was conceived!
Our Father also has a special mission for our little ones that each
one must accomplish. One that is considered important to God!

"For the gifts and the calling of God are irrevocable." *Romans 11:29*
He does not change His mind about those to whom He gives His grace
or to whom He sends His call.

Day 82

"Did not He who made me in the womb make him,
And the same one fashion us in the womb?" Job 31:15

We have all been created by God for HIS GLORY.
All of us count – whether we are an adult or an embryo!
Each person is loved and has a God-given dignity regardless
of gender, race, color, culture, or social standing.
For Our Lord has given each of us an eternal soul. He has adopted us
into His Heavenly Family to be His beloved children.
In His sight - we are all priceless.
We just have to choose to love Him back,
so we can go Home to spend eternal life with Our Father, when He
ordains it. We should not obstruct or stop
the plans God has for each of us.
We should not change or impede GOD's Divine Action of Creation.
We aren't God - nor should we PLAY 'god' with our decisions.
Seek Him – Seek His will – Seek His forgiveness & direction.
He will give you the grace to change & to follow Him.

Day 83

Behold, all souls are Mine; the soul of the father as
well as the soul of the son is Mine." *Ezekiel 18:4*

Every soul belongs to our heavenly Father. As Parents, we must respect
God's will and design for our child's life. Our responsibility is to give
our child a God-centered life, so that he/she will be equipped to
choose wisely to follow God's plan.

Description of a Worthy Father
A man whose heart is first centered on God's will, so
he can walk in: Integrity, Responsibility, and Nobility.
He is a man who desires to protect and guide his family.
His wife is cherished as his greatest gift on earth. And when God sends
children, the father receives them willingly from the hands of The Creator.

Day 84

*"Let us not lose heart in doing good, for in due time
we will reap if we do not grow weary." Galatians 6:9*

*God sees your heart. Your labors of love are not futile,
for it is in giving of yourself that you will find real freedom & true joy.
Take a minute to rest, and contemplate how the
Holy Spirit is working in and through you and how
your little one is being so miraculously formed!
Your baby is about 2 inches long now; his/her fingers will soon begin
to open and close, his toes will curl; his eye muscles will clench, and
his mouth will make sucking movements. Nerve cells are multiplying
rapidly, and in your baby's brain, synapses are forming rapidly.
God is blessing both of you tremendously, (even if this is unseen
for the moment) and He will continue to do so!*

Day 85

*"The disciples came to Jesus and said, 'Who then is greatest
in the kingdom of heaven?' Jesus called a child to Himself and
set him before them, and said, 'Truly I say to you, unless you are
converted and become like children, you will not enter the kingdom
of heaven. Whoever then humbles himself as this child,
he is the greatest in the kingdom of heaven." Matthew 18:1-4*

*Our Lord is clear that we should all be humble of mind & heart
just as little children are. Children are open, trusting, and eager to learn
and believe. Their enthusiasm, curiosity, and meekness allows the
Holy Spirit to work in them. As Jesus witnessed to us, we should all seek
to humble ourselves; this starts with thanking Him! Then in prayer,
with a contrite heart, we will see how to diminish our pride,
our self-oriented habits, and our need for worldly prestige.
Humility is the foundation of a healthy faith and an honest heart.*

Day 86

"Whoever receives one such child in My name receives Me." Matt.18:5

Our responsibility as parents is to encourage and nurture God's children to mature in faith & love for Him. A beautiful example of receiving a child in this love and faith is the example St. Joseph gave us. He listened to the Holy Spirit, even when he was tempted with doubts. He chose to say "Yes" to the very important mission entrusted to him. His God-given role in the Holy Family was to protect Our Lady and Baby Jesus, and to provide a home where Jesus could mature into an adult. St. Joseph is a wonderful example for fathers, step-fathers, and for couples that choose adoption.

"In protecting Jesus, in teaching him how to grow in age, wisdom and grace, St. Joseph's is a model for every educator and in particular for every father. I ask for you the grace to be ever closer to your children, allow them to grow, but be close, close! They need you, your presence, your closeness, your love. Be, for them, like St. Joseph: protectors of their growth in age, wisdom and grace; Guardians along their path." *Pope Francis*

Day 87

"See that you do not despise one of these little ones, for I say to you that their angels in heaven continually see the face of My Father who is in heaven." *Matthew 18:10*

*"The child is God's gift to the family. Each child is created in the special image and likeness of God for greater things –
To love and to be loved.
In this year of the family we must bring the child back to the center of our care and concern. This is the only way that our world can survive because our children are the only hope for the future."*
Mother Teresa of Calcutta

"Not only would I say that the family is important for the evangelization of the new world. *The family is important, and it is necessary for the survival of humanity.* **Without the family, the cultural survival of the human race would be at risk.** *The family, whether we like it or not, is the foundation."* *Pope Francis*

Day 88

*"It is not the will of your Father which is in heaven,
that one of these little ones should perish."* Matthew 18:14

This is a powerful Scripture! "Perish" has two meanings:
1. *To suffer death, typically in a violent, sudden, or untimely way*
2. *To go bad, go off in another direction, to spoil*

*In the first meaning: a life is lost, which God does NOT will. A life is
a life no matter how small. That life has a soul & will behold God.*
*In the second meaning: we should choose to follow God's plan. If we
take Him out of our life, we will "go off in another direction" – without
Him. In doing so, in choosing our own way – we leave God – and make
our **Self** into a god. Think about that. You are with HIM, or you are not!*

*St. Augustine reminds us: "God loves each one of us,
as if there were only one of us!"*

Day 89

*"Be devoted to one another in brotherly love;
in honor give preference to one another."* Romans 12:10

*"Do not think that love in order to be genuine
has to be extraordinary. What we need is to
love without getting tired.
Be faithful in small things because it is in
Them that your strength lies.
We cannot do great things.
We can only do little things with great love."
Mother Teresa of Calcutta*

*"Let us do good while we still have time, and we will
render glory to our heavenly Father, sanctify ourselves,
and give good example to others."* St. Padre Pio

Day 90

"Beyond all these things put on love,
Which is the perfect bond of unity." Colossians 3:14

Love never fails to keep us in accord with God's will and with the full
life He has designed for us. Your baby is, and will continue to be, an
incredible GIFT; one that will bring an immense dimension of love
to your life that you will always remember and cherish.
As you grow with your child, you will also find yourself closer to
God's love, as you contemplate your Creator's generosity. Suddenly, you
will find yourself giving more completely; in fact, it will become a natural
occurrence. As an extra bonus, you will receive from your child the
most tender hugs and kisses– that you could ever imagine.
"Now faith, hope and love abide - these three; but
the greatest of these is love." 1 Corinthians 13:13

Day 91

"As those who have been chosen of God, holy and beloved,
put on a heart of compassion, kindness, humility,
gentleness and patience." Colossians 3:12

"All of us give credit to our mothers for life and many other things,
but not always are they listened to or helped in everyday life...Their
important contribution to the life of society, their daily sacrifices, and
their aspirations are not always properly appreciated.
To be a mother is a gift. Through their sacrifices, mothers assist in
helping society to overcome its self-centered tendencies, as well as its lack
of openness, generosity and concern for others. In this sense motherhood
is more than childbearing; it is a life choice entailing sacrifice, respect
for life, and commitment to passing on those human and religious
values which are essential for a healthy society," Pope Francis

Day 92

"Therefore be imitators of God, as beloved children;
and walk in love, just as Christ also loved you and gave Himself up
for us, an offering and a sacrifice to God as a fragrant aroma.
Wives, be subject to your own husbands, as to the Lord.
For the husband is the head of the wife, as Christ also is the head
of the church, He Himself being the Savior of the body. But as
the church is subject to Christ, so also the wives ought to be to
their husbands in everything." Ephesians 5:1-2, 22-24

"St. Paul is putting an emphasis on mutuality & always giving
thanks; the use of Old Testament Commandment to honor your
father and mother (Eph 6:2); and above all the initial principle
of subordination to one another under Christ, thus effectively
undermining exclusive claims to domination by one party. So,
regarding wives and husbands, this is an **elaborate teaching on**
the relationship between Christ and the church, one that has
been woven together!" *USCCB Commentary on Ephesians 5*

Day 93

"Husbands, love your wives, just as Christ also loved the church and gave Himself up for her, so that He might sanctify her, having cleansed her by the washing of water with the word, that He might present to Himself the church in all her glory, having no spot or wrinkle or any such thing; but that she would be holy and blameless. So husbands ought also to love their own wives as their own bodies. He who loves his own wife loves himself; for no one ever hated his own flesh, but nourishes and cherishes it, just as Christ also does the church, because we are members of His body." Ephesians 5:25-30

*"St. Paul exhorts married Christians to a strong mutual love. Holding with Gen 2:24, that **marriage is a divine institution** (Eph 5:31), St. Paul sees Christian marriage as taking on a new meaning symbolic of the intimate relationship of love between Christ and the church. **The wife should serve her husband in the same spirit as that of the church's service to Christ** (Eph 5:22, 24), and **the husband should care for his wife with the devotion of Christ to the church** (Eph 5:25–30). St. Paul gives to the Genesis passage its highest meaning in the light of the union of Christ and the church, of which Christ like loyalty and devotion in Christian marriage are a clear reflection."* USCCB Commentary on Ephesians 5

Fourth Month
(14-17 weeks)

The Second Trimester of your pregnancy has begun (**fourth, fifth, and sixth months**), and hopefully you will lose some of the First Trimester symptoms, such as nausea and fatigue. In fact, you may have an increased appetite as your abdomen expands and the baby grows. During the fourth month of your pregnancy, your baby will develop eyebrows, eyelashes, and fingernails. The outer ear will also develop and your baby will hear your heartbeat, your voice, and other external noises. You may feel slight movement as your baby stretches his/her arms and legs. A fine downy hair called *lanugo* will begin to grow on your baby's face and body. The baby will also be covered with a waxy coating for protection as it floats in the amniotic fluid within the sac.

By the end of the fourth month, your baby will grow rapidly to be six to seven inches long and weigh five ounces. Drink plenty of water; the umbilical cord is transporting 300 quarts of fluids per day!

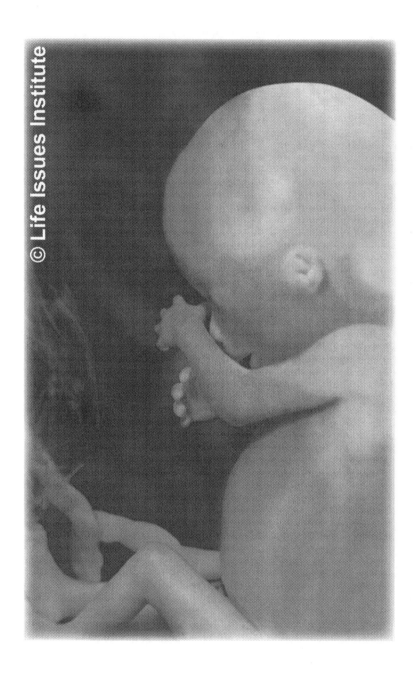

Day 94

"For it is God who is at work in you, both to will and to work for His good pleasure." *Philippians 2:13*

"The Church' desires to give thanks to the Most Holy Trinity
for the 'mystery of woman' and for every woman - for all
that constitutes the eternal measure of her feminine dignity,
for the 'great works of God', which throughout human history
have been accomplished in and through her."
"Thank you, women who are mothers!"
"Thank you, women who are wives!"
"Thank you, every woman,
for the simple fact of being a woman!"
"Through the insight which is so much a part of your womanhood, you
enrich the world's understanding and help to make human relations
more honest and authentic." Pope Saint John Paul II, Letter to Women

Day 95

"All things were created by Him, both in the heavens and on earth, visible and invisible, ... all was created through Him and for Him. He is before all things, and in Him all things hold together." *Colossian 1:16b-17*

The Purpose of our Existence

"Unless we have something of supreme value, something at the center of
our being which we can venerate, human beings gradually deteriorate.
Human nature is so constituted that it must have something holy that it
can worship, otherwise something else will take its place. God & His
Word should evoke and receive - great veneration, praise, reverence, and
awe. We must believe in the truth at the center of our being, which is
the purpose of our existence. We must also bear testimony to
this belief by the proper fulfillment of our life's purpose."

Father Alfred Delp, S.J.
Father Delp was condemned to death by the Nazis in Berlin, Germany

Day 96

*"Upon Thee I was cast from birth; Thou has
been my God from my mother's womb." Psalm 22:10*

*Heavenly Father, please help me to fulfill the special purpose
You have for my life, that I may show my gratitude & esteem to You!
I thank you for your faithfulness every day of my life. I recognize that
it is an honor to be a parent; to COOPERATE with YOU in bringing
a precious being & a priceless soul into this world.*

*Thank You, Father, for loving each of us into being.
Please guide me as I care for the special life within me –
a life You have entrusted to me. What confidence You must have in me.
Please equip me to be my best for this cherished soul of yours.
I know You to be a Generous God who will provide for us.
I now understand why we have eternity – to have enough time
to thank You for all your incredible blessings.*

Day 97

*"It will be told of the Lord to the coming generation.
They will come and will declare His righteousness
To a people who will be born, that
He has performed wondrous works." Psalm 22:30-31*

*Tell the coming generation of God's greatness, of His loyalty, of
His merciful heart, and of His unconditional love & sacrifices for us.*

"Through the grace of the sacrament of marriage, parents receive
the responsibility and privilege of evangelizing their children.
Parents should initiate their children at an early age into the mysteries
of the faith of which they are the *"first heralds"* for their children.
They should associate them from their tenderest years with the life
of the Church. A wholesome family life can foster interior dispositions
that are a genuine preparation for a *living faith* and remain a
support for it throughout one's life." *CCC 2225*

Day 98

**"We have obtained an inheritance, having been predestined
according to His purpose who works all things after the
Counsel of His will."** *Ephesians 1:11*

*According to God's will, we receive redemption and forgiveness
of our sins through Jesus Christ. If we are faithful followers, we will
be rewarded with an eternal life with Our Lord. Your baby has also
received this promise, so teach your child the principles of our faith, that
we may all be one Family in Heaven.*

**"No eye has seen, no ear has heard
and no one's heart has imagined
all the things that God has prepared
for those who love him."** *1 Corinthians 2:9*

Day 99

**"What shall I render to the LORD
For all His benefits toward me?"** *Psalm 116:12*

**"Good, better, best.
Never let it rest.
Til your good is better
And your better is best."**
Saint Ignatius of Loyola

*"Be careful to listen to all these words which I command you, so that
it may be well with you and your sons after you forever, for you will
be doing what is good and right in the sight of
the Lord your God."* *Deuteronomy 12:28*

"Be strong in the grace that is in Christ Jesus. Suffer hardship with *me*,
as a good soldier of Christ Jesus. Consider what I say, for the Lord
will give you understanding in everything." *2 Timothy 2:1, 3, 7*

Day 100

*"Gracious is the L*ORD*, and righteous;*
Yes, our God is compassionate.
*The L*ORD *preserves the humble;*
I was brought low, and He saved me.
Return to your rest, O my soul,
*For the L*ORD *has dealt bountifully with you."* Psalm 116:5-7

"Sometimes the soul is distinguished from the spirit: St. Paul
for instance prays that God may sanctify his people "wholly", with
"spirit and soul and body" kept sound and blameless at the Lord's
coming. The Church teaches that this distinction does not introduce a
duality into the soul. "Spirit" signifies that from creation man is ordered
to a **supernatural end and that his soul can gratuitously be raised**
beyond all it deserves to Communion with God." *CCC 367*

Day 101

"Know brethren, beloved by God,
That He has chosen you." 1 Thessalonians 1:4

Out of God's great love and wisdom,
He chose you to come into being.
He also chose your baby to come into being.
God never makes an error in His choice. Choose God!

"I endure all things for the sake of those who are chosen,
so that they also may obtain the salvation which is in Christ Jesus
and with it eternal glory. It is a trustworthy statement:
For if we died with Him, we will also live with Him;
If we endure, we will also reign with Him;
If we deny Him, He also will deny us;
If we are faithless, He remains faithful,
For He cannot deny Himself." 2 Tim. 2:10-13

Day 102

"There was a man in Jerusalem whose name was Simeon; and this man was righteous and devout, looking for the consolation of Israel; and the Holy Spirit was upon him. And it had been revealed to him by the Holy Spirit that he would not see death before he had seen the Lord's Christ. And he came in the Spirit into the temple; and when the parents brought in the child Jesus, to carry out for Him the custom of the Law, Simeon then took Him into his arms, and blessed God, and said, 'Now Lord, Thou does let Thy bond-servant depart in peace, according to Thy word; For my eyes have seen Thy salvation.'" Luke 2:25-30

*Through the Holy Spirit, Simeon perceives not only a baby before him, but that this Baby is the answer to God's covenant with His people. Simeon's spirit is led to discern that **Baby Jesus is the Promised One**. We all need to recognize God's presence in every life: their unique calling and how that person will touch other lives as Our Lord has ordained.*

Day 103

"I will have compassion on her who had not obtained compassion, And I will say to those who were not My people, 'You are My people!' And they will say, 'You are my God!'" Hosea 2:23

*We have all fallen short and need God's mercy. All of us have weaknesses & strengths. Perhaps you are stuck thinking, 'I am a miserable sinner who is condemned'. We may have a difficult time forgiving ourselves for our worst act; however, **Our Lord does give us a Second Chance,** when we are contrite. Ask forgiveness, and God will renew you. Never lose hope, nor feel unworthy to reach out to God. He wants us to persevere in asking and seeking Him. God is love; He wants us to love Him with our whole heart. Our God is a NOBLE GOD; He is gracious and merciful! He awaits our return home with outstretched arms. **Now is the time to seek Him even more, for yourself & for the sake of your Little One. To start all fresh & new!** May you grow in the assurance of your faith and love for God, so you will be equipped to pass on the baton to the next generation.*

Day 104

"The foolishness of God is wiser than men, and the weakness of God is stronger than men. For consider your calling, brethren, that there were not many wise according to the flesh, not many mighty, not many noble; but God has chosen the foolish things of the world to shame the wise, and God has chosen the weak things of the world to shame the things which are strong, that no man may boast before God." 1 Cor. 1:25-27, 29

"I believe though I do not comprehend, and I hold by faith what I cannot grasp with the mind." St. Bernard

"David, Samuel, and the prophets by faith conquered kingdoms, performed acts of righteousness, obtained promises, shut the mouths of lions, quenched the power of fire, & escaped the edge of the sword; from their weakness they were made strong, became mighty in war, and put foreign armies to flight." Hebrews 11:32b-34

Day 105

"For whoever does the will of My Father who is in heaven, he is My brother and sister and mother." Matthew 12:50

"Those who choose to walk in faith, love, and obedience to God's laws are Members of the Family of God. We must remember and know that **when we call God 'Our Father' We ought to behave as sons of God."** *Saint Cyprian*

"Ask Jesus to make you a saint. After all, only He can do that. Go to Confession regularly and to Communion as often as you can." Saint Dominic Savio Saint at age 14

Day 106

**"I pray that the eyes of your heart may be enlightened, so that
you will know what is the hope of His calling, what are the riches of
the glory of His inheritance in the saints, and what is the surpassing
greatness of His power toward us who believe."** *Ephesians 1:18-19a*

*"My Lord and my God, take from me
everything that distances me from you.
My Lord and my God, give me everything that brings me closer to you.
My Lord and my God, detach me from myself to give my all to you."*
St. Nicholas of Flue

*We are here not just for our betterment,
but also for the betterment of others.*

**"I urge you therefore, brothers, by the mercies of God, to offer
your bodies as a living sacrifice, holy and pleasing to God,
your spiritual worship."** *Romans 12:1*

Day 107

**"He will be like a tree firmly planted by streams of water,
Which yields its fruit in its season and its leaf does not wither;
and in whatever he does, he prospers."** *Psalm 1:3*

*God wants us to flourish as we grow in His will. He increase our
understanding and He multiplies His blessings for our family.
As an expectant Mother & expectant Father,
enrich your spirits with God's Word,
and entrust yourselves & your baby to His care.
God's Word gives Life! God's Heart gives Devotion!*

*Mom may be feeling some kicks now! In fact your baby can turn
somersaults, so you may feel that turn or even a hiccup. Soon you will
be able to identify an elbow or head bulging at your sides.
These maternal movement of your baby bring so much Joy!*

Day 108

"Your wife shall be like a fruitful vine
Within your house,
Your children like olive plants
Around your table." Psalm 128:3

Holy Scripture always depicts Children as a GIFT and as a Blessing,
given by God to the parents. God is offering His love to the parents
through their baby. Hopefully, the parents will then offer this
love back to their child and to God - their Creator.
The LOVE parents give each other and give to their children,
is the Foundation of a Fruitful Family Life!

"God has not destined us for wrath, but to obtain salvation through
our Lord Jesus Christ, who died for us ... so that we will live together
with Him. Therefore encourage one another and
build up one another." *1 Thessalonians 5:9-11*

Day 109

"May you see your children's children." Psalm 128:6

What a blessing children are!
They bring so much love and joy into our lives;
And they teach us so much about God's love!
Children enrich our lives and bring the best out of us.
Just think what a delight it will also be
When we see our Grandchildren!
Build a Legacy of Love for your Future!
We only have one life to live - one life to love.

Fight for their future – through a Culture of Life!
Don't fear, God has always provided – generation after generation.
He promises goodness & always builds us up. He is a generous Creator.

Day 110

*"Grandchildren are the crown of old men,
and the glory of sons is their fathers."* Proverbs 17:6

*We work hard to provide for our family and to obtain what is necessary
for their future. However, remember how much more important
it is to take the time to show your children, and then your
grandchildren, how very special they are to us and to God. Then
your future will be crowned with beautiful memories, and a
peace in knowing that you directed wisely and gave your all!*

*"When you live in holiness, when you really try to stop sinning,
you become braver. You become more courageous,
and you become a man of your word.
You become a man of conviction
that you're not willing to sell out - and you're really
A true knight in shining armor."* Jim Caviezel, Actor

Day 111

*King David said, "As for you, my son Solomon, **know the God
of your father, and serve Him with a whole heart and a willing mind**;
for the LORD searches all hearts, and understands every intent of
our thoughts. **If you seek Him, He will let you find Him**; but if
you forsake Him, He will reject you forever."* 1 Chronicles 28:9

*What is it that you admire and respect in those that you look up to?
Is it their strong character and the virtues that reflect their loyal
faith in God? Ask God to illuminate your spirit, heart, and mind.
Then seek Him with your whole heart & a willing mind.
The seven virtues are: prudence, justice, temperance,
courage (or fortitude), faith, hope, and love.*

*"Now may the God of peace Himself sanctify you entirely; and may
your spirit and soul and body be preserved complete, without blame at
the coming of our Lord Jesus Christ."* 1 Thessalonians 5:23

Day 112

"Create in me a clean heart, O God,
And renew a steadfast spirit within me.
Do not cast me away from Your presence
And do not take Your Holy Spirit from me.
Restore to me the joy of Your salvation,
And sustain me with a willing spirit." Psalm 51:10-12

There are days when we may perceive ourselves as being
on Top of the World, and consequently we may forget to pray. Then there
are other days, when we just can't find the strength to take another step.
Whether we believe that we are on the top of a mountain or down in the
valley, we must continually persevere to ask Our Lord to renew our
heart & spirit: "Create in me a clean heart, O God, and renew
a steadfast spirit within me".

We can't stay in tune without His daily guidance and love!

Day 113

"Store up for yourselves treasures in heaven, where neither moth nor
rust destroys, and where thieves do not break in or steal; For where
your treasure is, there your heart will be also." Matthew 6:20-21

If we spend more time praying and reading the Holy Scriptures, we
will grow closer to God. Ask the Lord to help you grow in His holy
virtues and in the Fruit of the Spirit. These are everlasting treasures!

"The Holy Scriptures are our letters from Home." Saint Augustine

"We cultivate a very small field for Christ, but we love it, knowing
that God does not require great achievements but a heart that
holds back nothing for itself." St. Rose Phillipine Duchesne

Day 114

"Wait for the LORD;
Be strong and let your heart take courage;
Yes, wait for the LORD." Psalms 27:14

*I use to say this Psalm every day – to grow in **courage & patience***
because I felt so lost and miserable then. Then I grew - only
thanks to God being so Gracious & Faithful!
Keep your heart and soul in a state of peaceful expectation;
Wait on the LORD!

"The Fruit of the Spirit is love, joy, peace, patience, kindness,
goodness, faithfulness, gentleness, and self-control." Galatians 5:22-23

"Is not your awe & reverence of God
your source of confidence;
and the integrity of your ways your hope? Job 4:6

Day 115

"They will not labor in vain,
Or bear children for calamity;
For they are the offspring of those blessed by the LORD,
And their descendants with them". Isaiah 65:23

What a powerful acclamation of Hope!
Our Lord proclaims His faithfulness and His blessings,
especially to those who honor His will.
Keep your heart set on Him and you will not be disappointed.
God keeps His word! And His blessings for your faithfulness will
extend to your descendants, for His generosity cannot be outdone!

"Your loving kindness, O Lord, extends to the heavens,
Your faithfulness reaches to the skies." Psalm 36:5

Day 116

"The Child continued to grow and become strong, increasing
in wisdom; and the grace of God was upon Him." Luke 2:40

The seven Gifts of the Holy Spirit are: wisdom, understanding,
counsel, fortitude, knowledge, piety, and fear (awe) of the Lord.

In the course of our daily life we are confronted with decisions that
we must make. As believers we need to be equipped in our minds and
hearts to choose wisely, especially when there is so much confusion.
The seven Gifts of the Holy Spirit complete and perfect the virtues
we need to be growing in - to follow Christ's perfect plan for us.

"Teach me to do Your will, for You are my God;
Let Your good Spirit lead me on a level path." Ps 143:10

"For all who are led by the Spirit of God are sons of God...
If children, then heirs, heirs of God and
fellow heirs with Christ." Romans 8:14, 17

Day 117

"Behold, I am the Lord, the God of all flesh;
Is anything too difficult for Me?" Jeremiah 32:27

Why hesitate to place your burdens before God?
Isn't HE the One - who fashioned us all?
Doesn't He manage every detail of our great universe?
He is the great "I AM"!
He is here for us NOW. He is a Living and True God!
Is anything too difficult for HIM?
In college I enjoyed studying geology because I saw God's genius in
His creation. One rare mineral that amazed me was a staurolite.
The atoms actually line up in a cruciform twinning of two
prismatic crystals, forming a cross at 60 degree angles. The
fact that God has these iron aluminum silicate atoms bond
and line up with such perfect dimensions, structure
and axial elements - to form a cross is an incredible masterpiece!
No wonder our Lord said, "I tell you, if these become silent, the stones
will cry out (to His glory)!" Luke 19:40

Day 118

"For I hope in You, O Lᴏʀᴅ;
You will answer, O Lord my God." Psalm 38:15

Would a parent ignore the needs of their child?
Most parents want to give their very best to their child (children).
Likewise, our Heavenly Father hears the prayers of His children, and
knows their many concerns and needs. *God does want to give each of
us His Best; so He attends to our needs **according to His will for our
life.** We must trust Him that He has the very best design for our lives!*
The answer may not be exactly what we thought of, *but God knows what
will work*; what will help us grow and mature towards HIM! We must be
confident of the fact that Our Lord does hear us, and that His answers are
what we need. His decisions are made with *The Utmost Love & Wisdom.*
**"I would have despaired unless I had believed that I would see
the goodness of the Lᴏʀᴅ in the land of the living."** *Psalm 27:13*

Day 119

"In hope against hope he believed,
So that he might become a father of many nations
According to that which had been spoken,
"Sᴏ sʜᴀʟʟ ʏᴏᴜʀ ᴅᴇsᴄᴇɴᴅᴀɴᴛs ʙᴇ." Romans 4:18

In hope and faith Abraham believed God's promise.
His strong faith was rewarded with many descendants,
through whom God's promise was realized.

**"Believing is an act of the intellect assenting to the Divine truth by
command of the will, moved by God through grace."** *St Thomas Aquinas*

Ask for more grace in your life – especially when tempted to doubt.
It is in "hope against hope" that we persevere and win the race.
"Run in such a way that you may win." *1 Corinthians 9:24b*

Day 120

"Hope does not disappoint, because the love of God has been poured out within our hearts through the Holy Spirit Who was given to us." Romans 5:5

"Hope is practiced through the virtue of patience, which continues to do good even in the face of apparent failure, and through the virtue of humility, which accepts God's mystery and trusts him even at times of darkness."
Pope Benedict XVI, God Is Love--Deus Caritas Est.

God does not keep us festering in discouragement; He waits for us and then gives us the necessary grace to get back on our feet.
"He loves, He hopes, He waits. If He came down on our altars on certain days only, some sinner, on being moved to repentance, might have to look for Him, and not finding Him, might have to wait. Our Lord prefers to wait Himself for the sinner for years - rather than keep him waiting one instant." St. Peter Julian Eymard

Day 121

"Thus says the LORD, your Redeemer, *and The One who formed you from the womb, 'I, the LORD, am the maker of all things, Stretching out the heavens by Myself And spreading out the earth all alone.'"* Isaiah 44:24

As our eyes behold the Lord's grandeur, we should be in awe of all the splendor and wonder of God's creation - of our earth and of all the heavens above. God's glory and majesty should stir our hearts to be humble and grateful before our Maker.
Our Creator, who made everything - values us so much, and above all He created, that He chose to redeem us at a very great price. He could have made us **indebted servants for all He has done for us**, *but instead He gives us the respect & dignity of a free will! Amazing!*
He lets us choose Him; He lets us choose to love Him! He never forces us!

Day 122

"For I am the LORD your God, who upholds your right hand,
Who says to you, 'Do not fear, I will help you.'" Isaiah 41:13

"The man who does not enter into himself, nor keeps God before
his eyes, is easily moved with a word of blame. Whereas he that
trusts in Me, and has no desire to stand by his own judgment,
shall be free from the fear of men."
Thomas à Kempis

*Don't get caught up in **our culture's definition of respect** - which is*
'going along with the crowd', i.e. feeling esteem from people. This peer
pressure will stunt your heart to truth and will change your values, since
you will be centered on "man" and will then fear 'not to disappoint' your
"friends(?)". Don't conform to the world - Keep God FIRST in your life!

"My help comes from the Lord, Who made heaven and earth." Ps. 121:2

Day 123

"Do not call to mind the former things,
or ponder things of the past.
Behold, I will do something new,
Now it will spring forth; Will you not be aware of it?
I will even make a roadway in the wilderness,
Rivers in the desert." Isaiah 43:18-19

This verse overwhelms me with gratitude for God. I remember when my
days were so difficult and I was so alone, that I had no "roadway in the
wilderness" nor an inkling of how to solve so many problems. Yet God
reached out & touched me with His light! His Spirit of unconditional love
and compassion - touched my spirit and restored my soul. I could not
*have made it otherwise. **I owe all to Him – for He does create us anew!***
He did help me to find the correct course for
LIFE! He is there for you too!
"O Lord, You are our Father, We are the clay, and You our potter;
and all of us are the work of Your hand". Isaiah 64:8

Day 124

"The people whom I formed for Myself
will declare My praise." Isaiah 43:21

Those who serve the Lord with their whole heart will
grow strong in the Spirit, because they have examined
their soul and have chosen to please God
rather than man. Spiritual progress always enlightens
Our true devotion!

"Am I now seeking the favor of men, or of God?
Or am I striving to please men? If I were still trying to please men,
I would not be a servant of Christ." Galatians 1:10

"For they loved the glory & the approval of men,
rather than the approval and glory of God." John 12:43

"Stop regarding man, whose breath of life is in his nostrils;
For why should he be esteemed?" Isaiah 2:22

Fifth Month
(18-22 weeks)

Your baby will grow to be 7 to 10 inches long, and weigh about 10 to 12 ounces. This is a period of tremendous growth for your baby. Your baby is also growing muscle and is getting stronger every day. As your baby becomes stronger, he will move about more energetically. *This movement is such a great maternal feeling, to feel your little one move inside you!*
Eyebrows, eyelids, and eyelashes will appear. Your baby's brain will be developing a lot this month. The number of nerve cells will increase rapidly, particularly in the front of the brain, where thinking takes place. At times you may feel a shortness of breath as the baby grows larger. Your body will compensate naturally by breathing deeper and more frequently – this is all normal. By the end of this month, you will be more visibly pregnant and will probably feel more comfortable in maternity clothes. It may be more comfortable for you to eat frequent, smaller meals, versus three large meals.

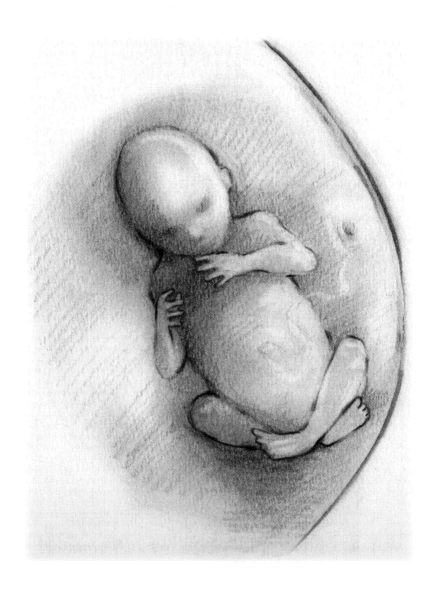

Day 125

"For this child I prayed, and the Lord *has given me my petition which I asked of Him. So I have dedicated him to the* Lord*; as long as he lives he is dedicated to the Lord."* 1 Samuel 1:27-28

This is a beautiful prayer to use while praying over your baby.
Yes, start praying now for your little one (if you haven't already).
As Hannah dedicated her son, Samuel, to the Lord – you may also want
to dedicate your child's life to God. Ask the Lord to direct your child's
spiritual growth all of his/her life. May you and your child grow in
faith and love to **Be of Service** *in His Kingdom.*
May the Lord protect you and your Family
And keep you in His ways.

How precious is Your loving kindness, O God! The children
of men take refuge in the shadow of Your wings. *Psalm 36:7*

Day 126

"For what thanks can we render to God for you
in return for all the joy with which we rejoice before
our God on your account?" I Thessalonians 3:9

How can we adequately thank God for the gift of a new life?
God is truly generous and loving beyond all measure. A new life is
His bestowment of love and grace on us. It is also a special opportunity
to grow and share in a beautiful relationship of unconditional
love and joy - between God, the child, and the parents.
It is an invitation to be someone extraordinary
to someone extraordinary.

"They shall eagerly utter the memory of Your abundant goodness
And will shout joyfully of Your righteousness." Psalms 145:7
"Oh give thanks to the Lord, call upon His name;
Make known His deeds among the people." 1 Chronicles 16:8

Day 127

"Now the man had relations with his wife Eve, and she conceived and gave birth to Cain, and she said, 'I have begotten a man child with the help of the LORD.'" Genesis 4:1

*"When a new person is born of the conjugal union of the two, he brings with him into the world a particular image and likeness of God himself: the genealogy of the person is inscribed in the very biology of generation. In affirming that the spouses, as parents, cooperate with God the Creator in conceiving and giving birth to a new human being, we are not speaking merely with reference to the laws of biology. Instead, we wish to emphasize that **God himself is present in human fatherhood and motherhood** quite differently than he is present in all other instances of begetting 'on earth'. Indeed, **God alone is the source of that 'image and likeness' which is proper to the human being,** as it was received at Creation. Begetting is the continuation of Creation."*
Letter to Families, Pope Saint John Paul II

Day 128

"I will give God thanks with all my heart." Psalm 138a

"Thank you, *women who are mothers!* You have sheltered human beings within yourselves in a unique experience of joy and travail. This experience makes you become *God's own smile upon the newborn child,* the one who guides your child's first steps, who helps it to grow, and who is the anchor as the child makes its way along the journey of life. Thank you, *women who are wives!* You irrevocably join your future to that of your husbands, in a relationship of *mutual giving,* at the service of love & life. Thank you, *every woman,* for the simple fact of being *a woman!* Through the insight which is so much a part of your womanhood you enrich the world's understanding *and help to make human relations more honest and authentic.* When it comes to setting women free from every kind of exploitation and domination, *the Gospel* contains an ever relevant message which goes back to the *attitude of Jesus Christ himself.* Transcending the established norms of his own culture, *Jesus treated women with openness, respect, acceptance and tenderness.* In this way Jesus honored the dignity *which women have always possessed according to God's plan & in His love."*
Letter to Women, Pope Saint John Paul II

Day 129

"Be strong and courageous! Do not tremble or be dismayed, for the LORD your God is with you wherever you go." Joshua 1:9

"Yes, it is time to *examine the past with courage,* to assign responsibility where it is due in a review of the long history of humanity. Women have contributed to that history as much as men and, more often than not, they did so in much more difficult conditions. What great appreciation must be shown to those women who, with a *heroic love for the child* they have conceived,… and proceeded with the pregnancy. Here we are thinking … also of societies which are blessed by prosperity and peace, and yet are often *corrupted by a culture of hedonistic permissiveness* which aggravates tendencies to aggressive male behavior. In these cases the choice to have an abortion always remains a grave sin. But before being something to blame on the woman, it is a crime for which guilt needs to be attributed to men and to the complicity of the general social environment."

Letter to Women, Pope Saint John Paul II

Day 130

"Then the LORD God said, 'It is not good for the man to be alone; I will make him a helper suitable for him.'" Genesis 2:18

"The creation of woman is thus marked from the outset by
The principle of help: a help which is not one-sided but *mutual.*
Woman complements man, just as man complements woman:
men and women are *complementary.*
Womanhood expresses the 'human' as much as
manhood does, but in a different and complementary way.
It is only through the duality of the 'masculine' and
the 'feminine' that the 'human' *finds full realization."*

Pope Saint John Paul II, Letter to Women,

*"God saw all that He had made, and behold,
it was very good." Genesis 1:31*

Day 131

"Delight yourself in the LORD;
And He will give you the desires of your heart." Psalm 37:4

*"The Beatitudes respond **to the natural desire for happiness.***
This desire is of divine origin: God has placed it in the human
***heart** in order to draw man to the One who alone can fulfill it:*
We all want to live happily; in the whole human race
there is no one who does not assent to this proposition,
even before it is fully articulated." CCC 1718
"How is it, then, that I seek you, Lord? Since in seeking you,
my God, I seek a happy life, let me seek you so that my soul
may live, for my body draws life from my soul and my soul
*draws life from you. **God alone satisfies.**" Saint Augustine*

Day 132

"Commit your way to the LORD,
Trust also in Him, and He will do it." Psalm 37:5

"Let nothing disturb you,
Let nothing frighten you,
All things are passing away:
God never changes!
Patience obtains all things
Whoever has God lacks nothing;
God alone is enough." Santa Teresa de Avila

*"**Consider it all joy, my brethren, when you encounter various trials,***
knowing that the testing of your faith produces endurance. And
let endurance have its perfect result, so that you may be perfect
***and complete, lacking in nothing.**" James 1:2-4*
"His Majesty, Our Lord, rewards great services with
trials, and there can be no better reward, for out of
trials springs love for God." Santa Teresa de Avila

Day 133

"The very hairs of your head are all numbered." Matthew 10:30

The fact that Our Lord knows and cherishes every detail about us - shows us how much He cherishes us. Every detail about us is important to Him!

"Of all visible creatures only man is 'able to know and love his Creator'.
He is 'the only creature on earth that God has willed for its own sake',
and he alone is called to share, by knowledge and love, in God's own life.
It was for this end that he was created, and this is
the fundamental reason for his dignity:" CCC 356

"Thus says God the LORD,
Who created the heavens and stretched them out,
Who spread out the earth and its offspring,
Who gives breath to the people on it and spirit to those who walk
in it, "I am the LORD, *I have called You in righteousness,*
I will also hold You by the hand and watch over You." Isaiah 42:5-6a

Day 134

"Thou, O LORD, *does rule forever;*
Thy throne is from generation to generation." Lamentations 5:19

Mountains come and go; seas transgress and regress;
Civilizations flourish and perish;
Still Our Lord is steadfast and His Truth will endure forever!
He is constant – He is our Rock!

"Think back to the ancient generations and consider this:
has the Lord ever disappointed anyone who put his hope in
him? Has the Lord ever abandoned anyone who held him in
constant reverence? Has the Lord ever ignored anyone who
prayed to him? The Lord is kind and merciful; he forgives
our sins and keeps us safe in time of trouble." Sirach 2:10-11

Day 135

Peter and the apostles answered, "We must
obey God rather than men." Acts 5:29
Today it is easy to be confused, to be in a fog, or just "go
along to get along" with our world's standards or "social
norms". These ever changing fads; immoral precepts &
prejudices; and the "ideals" set up by society –
are energizing a few. In fact, we see people follow along with this
"peer respect' & "peer pressure" as if it had become their religion.
It appears that anything that they say will become the truth - for
that moment. (Tomorrow it will change). Please don't let your
ears be tickled by these lies- they will deceive and misdirect your
life! Let the Holy Spirit guide your CHOICES in life, to please
God - Not man! In the end we will all stand on our own before the
Lord, regardless of our background, position, race, or culture!
"For the time will come when they will not endure sound doctrine; but
wanting to have their ears tickled, they will accumulate for themselves
teachers in accordance to their own desires, and will turn away their
ears from the truth and will turn aside to myths." 2 Timothy 4:3-4

Day 136

"A Canaanite woman approached Jesus to ask Him
to help her daughter. Then Jesus said to her,
'O woman, your faith is great;
It shall be done for you as you wish.'
And her daughter was healed at once." Matthew 15:28

We should never be afraid, nor feel unworthy, to ask Our Lord for His
blessings on our family. It sometimes takes a bold and daring spirit
to take the first step in faith. Have the confidence to change; to move
forward and onward in faith. Your leap of faith will be rewarded!
"We have boldness and confidence through faith in Him." Ephes. 3:12
"Be strong, and let us show ourselves courageous for the sake
of our people and for the cities of our God; and may the
Lord do what is good in His sight." 2 Samuel 10:12

Day 137

"I can do all things through Him who strengthens me." Phil. 4:13

*Never doubt that God is a Living God, who **is here** with us.*
He is working in and through you. However, He is so noble and
respectful of your will – that even He - waits for you to call on Him!
God is always there to help us and build us up,
even if our faith is the size of a mustard seed.

"For truly I say to you, if you have faith the size of a mustard seed,
you will say to this mountain, 'Move from here to there,' and it
will move; and nothing will be impossible to you." Matthew 17:20

God will strengthen you during your pregnancy and later, as you raise
your child. Don't worry or focus on the world's culture or standards; don't
be dismayed. Trust God and let Him care for you
and the baby. Draw comfort and strength from your
Creator, Who loves and cares for both of you.

Day 138

"Who has performed and accomplished it,
Calling forth the generations from the beginning?
'I, the LORD, am the first, and with the last. I am He.'" Isaiah 41:4

All that has been created finds it beginning and end with Our Lord!
Your Baby is God's greatest work – built to spend eternity with
*his Maker. How gracious is our God **to offer us everything He has**.*

"I am the Alpha and the Omega, the first and the last,
The beginning and the end." Revelation 22:13

"Listen to the sermon preached to you by the flowers, the trees,
the shrubs, the sky, and the whole world. Notice how they preach to you
a sermon full of love, of praise of God, and how they invite you to glorify
the sublimity of that sovereign Artist who has given them being."
St. Paul of the Cross

Day 139

*"He chose us in Him before the foundation of the world,
that we would be holy and blameless before Him.
In love He predestined us to adoption as sons
through Jesus Christ to Himself,
according to the kind intention of His will."* Eph. 1:4-5

*In His loving will, God - Our Father, predestined us to
be His adopted children. In doing so, He chose to make the
Ultimate Sacrifice for us: to offer His only Son, Jesus Christ.
In offering His life for our salvation, Christ secured our place
as adopted sons in His Father's Kingdom. Our 'adoption' was paid
for by a very great sacrifice of love.* **"God is love"** *1 John 4:8*

*"You did not choose Me, but I chose you and appointed
you that you might go and bear fruit, and that your
fruit will last, so that whatever you ask
in My name, the Father will give you."* John 15:16

Day 140

*"I do not know how you came into being in my womb. It was not I
who gave you life and breath, nor I who set in order the elements
within each of you. Therefore the Creator of the world, who
shaped the beginning of man and devised the origin of all things,
will in His mercy give life and breath back to you again, since
you now will forget yourselves for the sake of his laws. . . Look at
the heaven and the earth and see everything that is in them, and
recognize that God did not make them out of things that existed.
Thus also mankind comes into being."* 2 Maccabees 7:22-23,28.
What a woman of Faith!

*This Mother watched the martyrdom of all seven of her sons who died
before her eyes, instead of breaking their **covenant relationship** with
God. They all **choose to be loyal to God FIRST!** They were told to eat
pork, which was forbidden. In refusing, each son was tortured and killed –
one by one before their Mother. They chose not to denounce their Faith.*

Day 141

"But as for me, I trust in You, O LORD,
and I say, 'You are my God.'
My times are in Your hand." Psalm 31:14-15a

Our days are determined by Our Creator. He knows the day of our birth and the day He will call us home. In His generosity, He has given us a free will to choose how we will live "This TIME".

"There is an appointed time for everything....
A time to give birth and a time to die." Ecclesiastes 3:1-2

"A person should take care into whose hands he entrusts himself, for as the master is, so will the disciple be;
And as the father is, so will be the son."
Saint John of the Cross

Day 142

Jesus said, "Everyone who hears these words of Mine, and acts on them, may be compared to a wise man who built his house upon the rock. And the rain fell, and the floods came, and the winds blew and slammed against that house; and yet it did not fall, for it had been Founded on the rock." Matthew 7:24-25

Act on these words! The best inheritance you can give your children is to build your house on the ROCK and to give them a foundation built on TRUTH! **In life we all carry our crosses, but we don't carry them alone because we HAVE a relationship with the Light of the world.**

Jesus says, "I am the way and the truth and the life." St. John 14:6

When Jesus spoke again to the people, he said,
"I am the light of the world. Whoever follows me will never walk in darkness, but will have the light of life." John 8:12

Day 143

*"Make me know Your ways, O L*ORD*; teach me Your paths." Psalm 25:4*

Dear Holy Spirit, please enlighten me as I
grow and mature in motherhood
(or fatherhood) with my developing baby. Please guide & direct us
along the way, that our lives may achieve the utmost You intended for us.

The Blessed Virgin Mary told Venerable Maria de Agreda
that she prayed this prayer every day:
"I gave Him thanks and praise for His immutable Being,
for His infinite perfections, and for having created me out of nothing;
acknowledging myself as His creature and the work of His hands,
I blessed Him and adored Him, giving Him honor for His magnificence
and Divinity, as the supreme Lord and Creator of myself and of all that
exits. I raised up my spirit to place it into His hands, offering myself with
profound humility and resignation to Him; asking Him to dispose of me
according to His will during that day and during all the days of my life,
and to teach me to fulfill whatever would be to His greater pleasure."

Day 144

"Like newborn babies, long for the pure milk of the word,
so that by it you may grow in respect to salvation." I Peter 2:2

Holy Scripture directs our hearts and actions to glorify God, because
the Word enlightens our hearts to know, love, and seek Our Lord's will.

"I will give thanks to You, O Lord my God, with all my heart,
And will glorify Your name forever." Psalm 86:12

"Christian, recognize your dignity and, now that you share in God's
own nature, do not return to your former base condition by sinning.
Remember who is your head and of whose body you are a member.
Never forget that you have been rescued from the power of darkness
and brought into the light of the Kingdom of God."
St. Leo the Great, Sermo 22 in nat. Dom., 3

Day 145

"Stand and consider the wondrous works of God." Job 37:14

Life abounds with God's great wonders!
Look about at His grandeur across the ocean blue;
at His delight in colorful, fragrant flowers; and at His delicate,
artistic snowflakes falling across majestic mountains.
As beautiful as they all are, can any of these 'wondrous works
of God', compare to the splendor and sparkle you will see
in your baby's smiling face?
Your Baby is God's most profound work!

"Man is the summit of the Creator's work." CCC 343

"Behold, children are a gift of the LORD,
The fruit of the womb is a reward." Psalm 127:3

Day 146

"I sought Your favor with all my heart;
Be gracious to me according to Your word." Psalm 119:58

All is grace – "For without Him we can do nothing".
"Indeed we also work, but we are only collaborating with God
who works, for His mercy has gone before us.
It has gone before us so that we may be healed, and follows
us so that once healed, we may be given life;
it goes before us so that we may be called,
and follows us so that we may be glorified;
it goes before us so that we may live devoutly,
and follows us so that we may always live with God:
For without Him we can do nothing.'"
St. Augustine, De Natura et Gratia, 31

We need God in our life - especially now as
He blesses us with more life!

Day 147

"For You have rescued my soul from death,
My eyes from tears, my feet from stumbling.
I shall walk before the Lord in the
land of the living." Psalm 116:8-9

We have all suffered from fear, sorrow, loneliness and confusion.
During these times it is very difficult to see clearly and to understand any
truth. It's also hard to look forward with hope to any sense of normalcy
or joy. We may feel like we are stuck in a whirlwind of unfavorable
circumstances - with no way out. Worst of all – we may feel that we
don't deserve God's love and forgiveness for our worst sins.
Keep seeking God – your true Father.
Our Good Shepherd is waiting to receive us back into the fold;
He waits for our heart to be true and contrite.
Trust Our Lord – He does bring light to our darkness,
hope to our despair, & His eternal love & mercy to heal
us & redirect us back to a new life with Him.
It is through this Great Love that our lives have meaning!

Day 148

"This will be written for the generation to come,
*That **a people yet to be created** may praise the Lord." Psalm 102:18*

This is an incredible Psalm – An Awesome Declaration:
"A people yet to be created"!
It promises: Future Children - Hope – Souls that will praise God!
Note God's intent: *His intent has always been to bless every generation!*
If God's love set our world in motion, then we are obviously held dear
in His Heart – from the very beginning! He created our beautiful world
for us with exquisite preparations. He is present and He will continue to
shower His blessings on His people. Our life is foremost in His planning.
Our life and our soul have a noble dignity from God that no one
can take from us. Each of us has a unique contribution to give.
So keep knocking, seeking, and searching for all that God wants to teach
you and lead you in. Directing our hearts back to Our Creator is the
utmost prize, that we may truly praise the Lord with a grateful heart!

Day 149

"O Lord, You have searched me and known me.
You know when I sit down and when I rise up;
You understand my thought from afar.
You scrutinize my path and my lying down,
And are intimately acquainted with all my ways." Psalm 139:1-3

God really knows YOU & He does care about everything that happens
to you. He also knows & cares for your Baby! He is ahead of you –
preparing the way for both of you. He knows the physical and emotional
changes and the demands you are experiencing now in your pregnancy.
He knows your concerns for the future. He is preparing a future of hope
& blessings for you and your baby - as you develop and grow together.
He has placed a special 'hedge of protection' around both of you.

"Have You not made a hedge of protection about him,
his house, and all that he has, on every side? You
have blessed the work of his hands." Job 1:10

Day 150

"Who satisfies your years with good things,
So that your youth is renewed like the eagle." Psalm 103:5

Keep an account of the days when the Lord lifts your spirit on high,
as if on eagle's wings! Hold on to those special moments of exuberance in
His Presence – when you know, that you know – that He touched your
soul! These memories lift us up, so we can carry on - even when the strain
of pregnancy or our daily commitments deplete us. God's Word will also
renew you when you are tempted to doubt or to feel despair.
"So will My Word be. I send it out, and it always
produces fruit. It shall accomplish all I desire and it
will prosper everywhere I send it." Isaiah 55:11

"Those who wait for the Lord will gain new strength;
They will mount up with wings like eagles,
They will run and not get tired,
They will walk and not become weary." Isaiah 40:31

Day 151

**"I will be a Father to you,
and you shall be sons and daughters to Me,"
says the Lord Almighty."** *II Corinthians 6:18*

*"Goals: The authentic masculine charism can be summed up
in one word - 'father'. All of the qualities of noble masculine
character, including strength, courage, discipline, initiative
and sacrifice, to name just a few, are brought
to bear in a father's vocation. The natural male impulse is to beget life.
Honorable men who are fathers (both physical and spiritual fathers) call
forth life, provide for life, and give both roots and wings to the
physical and spiritual life entrusted to their care."*
*"Now let's turn to what may be the most important element in the battle
for the male soul - allies. To be good fathers, men need brothers and
leaders. There is no substitute for the experience of knowing that men
who are surely your brothers in Christ walk beside you and behind you."*
"What's a Manly Man and How Can We Get More of Them?"
Fr. Robert Mc Teigue, SJ

Day 152

**"The Lord will be the stability of your times,
A wealth of salvation, wisdom and knowledge;
The fear of the LORD is his treasure."** *Isaiah 33:6*
*"Alone among all animate beings, man can boast of having been
counted worthy to receive a law from God: as an animal endowed with
reason, capable of understanding and discernment, he is to govern
his conduct by using his freedom and reason, in obedience to the One
who has entrusted everything to him."* *Tertullian (c. 160 - 240)*
**"Work out your salvation with fear and trembling;
for it is God who is at work in you, both to will and to
work for His good pleasure."** *Philippians 2:12-13*
**"I have not departed from the command of His lips; I have treasured
the words of His mouth more than my necessary food."** *Job 23:12*

Day 153

"I am the vine, you are the branches; he who abides in
Me and I in him, he bears much fruit, for apart from Me
you can do nothing." John 15:5

Our hearts have to be willing to listen and to receive God's
*Word and intent, so that we can **abide in Christ and bear fruit.***
With the correct disposition of mind and spirit we can then
***follow God's will.** Otherwise, the seed of faith that is sown will*
not take root; it will get scorched with the world's deceit.

Jesus spoke in parables, saying, "Behold, the sower went out
to sow; and as he sowed, some seeds fell beside the road, and
the birds came and ate them up. Others fell on the rocky places,
where they did not have much soil; and immediately they
sprang up, because they had no depth of soil. But when
the sun had risen, they were scorched; and because they had no root, they
withered away. Others fell among the thorns, and the thorns came up and
choked them out. And others fell on the good soil and yielded a crop,
some a hundredfold, some sixty, and some thirty." Matthew 13:3-8

Day 154

"He led forth His own people like sheep
And guided them in the wilderness like a flock;
He led them safely, so that they did not fear." Psalm 78:52-53a

Just as your developing baby is protected & provided for within
your womb, so will God's blessings continue to sustain your family
upon his/her birth. God does not abandon us. He would not bring us
into existence to deprive us - so that we then lose our way and perish.
"For you love all things that are and loathe nothing that you
have made; for you would not fashion what you hate.
How could a thing remain, unless you willed it; or be preserved,
had it not been called forth by you? But you spare all things,
because they are yours, O Ruler and Lover of souls, for your
***imperishable spirit is in all things!** Wisdom 11:24-12:1*

Day 155

*"The LORD is good; His loving kindness is everlasting
and His faithfulness to all generations." Psalm 100:5*

*God doesn't need us since He is complete and created all. All creation
started with Him. However, He does hope that we will be faithful in turn.*

*"The God who made the world and everything in it, being
Lord of heaven and earth, does not live in temples made
by man, nor is He served by human hands, as though he
needed anything, since He himself gives to all mankind
life and breath and everything." Acts 17:24-25*

*"To be a child means to owe one's existence to another,
and even in our adult life we never quite reach the point where
we no longer have to give thanks for being the person we are."
Hans Urs von Balthasar*

Sixth Month
(23-27 weeks)

Your Baby's skin has developed a protective fatty substance called
vernix. This greasy covering keeps the skin well lubricated and is
a good protection against skin infections. Your baby is about 9 to
10 inches in length now, and weighs approximately 1½ pounds.
Your baby's movements can be felt regularly now (a wonderful
motherly experience). The baby's bones which were relatively
soft and flexible, are beginning to harden with calcium deposits.
Fingerprints and toe prints are now visible. Eyelids will begin
to part, and the eyes will open occasionally for short periods of
time. Your baby will start to hear soon! Check with your Doctor
concerning prenatal exercises. These can help strengthen your back
muscles, and limber other muscles needed for labor and delivery.

Day 156

"The LORD called Me from the womb;
from the body of My mother He named Me." Isaiah 49:1b

The Archangel Gabriel foretold Christ's birth and His name,
for Our Father already knew the great plans He had for His Son.
God also knows what plans He has for each one of us. He already knows
who your baby is, and the path He hopes your little one will follow. In
God's wisdom, He hopes that we will all follow His will for our life and
that we will live a life full of blessings. Teach your child to know, love, and
serve His Heavenly Father. If we as parents decide to respect & follow
our Father's will – our children will then be equipped to choose wisely.

"Parents must regard their children as **children of God**
and respect them as *human persons*. Showing themselves obedient
to the will of the Father in heaven, they should educate
their children to fulfill God's law." CCC 2222

Day 157

"Jesus, knowing that all things had already been accomplished,
to fulfill the Scripture, said, 'I am thirsty.'" John 19:28

"When He was dying on the Cross, Jesus said, "I thirst."
Jesus is thirsting for our love, and this is the thirst of everyone,
poor and rich alike. We all thirst for the love of others that they
may go out of their way to avoid harming us and to do good to us.
This is the meaning of true love, to give until it hurts.
How do we persuade a woman not to have an abortion? As always,
we must persuade her with love and we remind ourselves that love
means to be willing to give until it hurts. Jesus gave even His life
to love us. So, *the mother* who is thinking of abortion, should
be helped to love, that is, *to give until it hurts her plans*, or her
free time, to *respect the life of her child. The father* of that
child, whoever he is, *must also give until it hurts*."
Mother Teresa of Calcutta

93

Day 158

"The Spirit Himself testifies with our spirit
that we are children of God." Romans 8:16

*"**God writes His name on the soul of every person.***
Reason and conscience are the God within us in the natural order.
Human beings are like so many books issuing from the Divine press,
and if nothing else be written on them, at least
the name of the Author is indissolubly engraved on the title page.
God is like the watermark on paper, which may be written over
without ever being obscured."
Archbishop Fulton Sheen, *Life of Christ*

We must live up to the great honor God has given us - to claim us as
His children. In gratitude to this incredible dignity, we should choose
to live and walk as faithful and loyal children who belong to the
'Author of Life'.
Commit your life and your baby to the Lord!

Day 159

"That the generation to come might know,
Even the children yet to be born,
That they may arise and tell them to their children,
That they should put their confidence in God
And not forget the works of God,
but keep His commandments." Psalm 78:6-7

Powerful Psalm & Testimony to God's Providence!
Remember this Scripture daily and consider these facts:
That God's Word still stands as Truth;
His promises are always fulfilled in wisdom, grace & mercy;
*that God has always known us – who we **would be;***
He has great plans for us; and He hopes we will proclaim
His great works to all generations -
To follow His commands & to put
our confidence in Our Loving Father.
Our free response to His graciousness brings
more graciousness & more richness in life!

Day 160

"Build houses and live in them;
and plant gardens and eat their produce.
Take wives and become the fathers of sons and daughters,
And take wives for your sons and give your daughters to husbands,
that they may bear sons and daughters; and multiply there
and do not decrease." Jeremiah 29:5-6

God wants us to continue – to increase – to build & live!
He wants us to work towards what really counts and has real value!
"Take wives and become fathers."
He is very clear about getting married and having children!
Keep striving & be strong in hope and perseverance!

"All life demands struggle. Those who have everything given to them
become lazy, selfish, and insensitive to the real values of life. The
very striving and hard work that we so constantly try to avoid is the
major building block in the person we are today." Pope Paul VI

Day 161

"Blessed are the pure in heart, for they shall see God." Matthew 5:8

"Living the good life as created beings depends on living within
the limits and according to the truths of the human condition.
Purity of heart and the capacity to channel desires toward personal
self-mastery in holiness are part of the high calling of the Christian life.
*These remain necessities, despite the promises of a **false humanism***
that claims that human nature has neither limits nor boundaries, being
infinitely plastic and malleable – it is a vain and counterproductive
attempt to liberate humans from guilt." George Cardinal Pell

To have a pure heart means that we must first live by the rules God
has established. This brings a moral purity and peace to our soul.
Our conscience will always bear witness to the truth that is written
in our heart, if we are listening. In addition, there are times when
we will have an unforgettable "God-given" experience that goes
beyond mere coincidence. We become aware of God through
an inner voice, where God really touches us with His presence.
An unforgettable moment - that will change you forever.

Day 162

"Be strong and very courageous; be careful to do all according to the law which Moses My servant commanded you; do not turn from it either to the right or to the left, so that you may have success wherever you go." Joshua 1:7

Rules of Conduct always set standards, address proper responsibility, set our minds on the truth, and direct our hearts to be noble. These rules are based on the natural law. According to St. Thomas Aquinas, natural law is "nothing else than the rational creature's participation in the eternal law". This eternal law is based on God's wisdom, which directs man's thoughts and actions to the highest good - God's will. "The natural law is written and engraved in the soul of each and every man, because it is human reason ordaining him to do good and forbidding him to sin . . . But this command of human reason would not have the force of law if it were not the voice and interpreter of a higher reason to which our spirit and our freedom must be submitted." Pope Leo XIII

Day 163

"He will restore the hearts of the fathers to their children, and the hearts of the children to their fathers." Malachi 4:6

The Heart of the Father
"God the Father's plan is to do extraordinary things in the lives of ordinary men. Our problem is that our expectations of what God wants to do to us, and through us as fathers - are too small. 'Joseph had the heart of a father bestowed on him by the Eternal Father in the sharing of their common name'. Centuries ago the prophet Malachi told us to expect something miraculous to happen in the hearts of fathers. **Can you dare to believe that God's desire is to place within you – The heart of a father as He did to Joseph?"**
Steve Wood, Family Life Center

"He who is worried and full of anxiety in his work does an offense to God and does not **say the Our Father from the heart.** *Let us accept purely and simply whatever God sends us, without being concerned or sad."*
St. Joseph Marello

Day 164

"Flee from these things, you man of God, and pursue righteousness, godliness, faith, love, perseverance and gentleness. Fight the good fight of faith; take hold of the eternal life to which you were called. Guard what has been entrusted to you, avoiding worldly and empty chatter and the opposing arguments of what is falsely called "knowledge"— which some have professed and thus gone astray from the faith. 1 Timothy 6:11-12, 20*

As parents, we are entrusted with a very special life to love and guide. The family roots of faith you give your child will provide an important foundation of spiritual growth for your child's soul. Remember, your baby will be looking up to you for protection and direction. Therefore, be responsible guardians of your children, and entrust their lives to the Lord and His Church. They need Our Lord and His Sacraments to grow. Parents should study Scripture & learn continuously about the faith to pass God's wisdom on.

Day 165

"For this reason I bow my knees before the Father, from whom every family in heaven and on earth derives its name, that He would grant you, according to the riches of His glory, to be strengthened with power through His Spirit in the inner man, so that Christ may dwell in your hearts through faith; and that you, being rooted and grounded in love, may be able to comprehend with all the saints what is the breadth and length and height and depth, and to know the love of Christ which surpasses knowledge, that you may be filled up to all the fullness of God." Ephesians 3:14-19*

*"**Married love** particularly reveals its true nature and nobility when we realize that it **takes its origin from God**, who "is love," [1] the Father "from whom every family in heaven and on earth is named." [2] Marriage, then, is far from being the effect of chance or the result of the blind evolution of natural forces. It is in reality the wise and provident institution of God the Creator, whose purpose was to affect in man His loving design. As a consequence, husband and wife, through that mutual gift of themselves, which is specific and exclusive to them alone, develop that union of two persons in which they **perfect one another, cooperating with God in the generation and rearing of new lives."** ([1] 1 Jn 4:8; [2] Eph 3:15); Pope Paul VI, HUMANAE VITAE*

Day 166

"Have I not commanded you? Be strong and courageous!
*Do not tremble or be dismayed, for the L*ORD *your God is*
with you wherever you go." Joshua 1:9

At times you may feel quite alone with all the changes going on within you
and around you during your pregnancy. Sometimes those feelings and
emotions can be overwhelming. Others may not really understand this
"new world" you are in! Every minute of the day your mind is on your
developing baby. Not only do you feel the baby's movements, but you
are quite aware of your body changes too – especially since your baby
precedes you all day long! **Enjoy the world of motherhood***: the joy when*
your baby moves; your loving and protective maternal feelings; your
need to nest and prepare; and your hope to grow more - to give your
very best possible care to your little one.

Always remember that you are never alone, for the Lord is always at your
side. Confide in Him. **Fathers, I am not forgetting you** *- it's just that you*
aren't physically pregnant. Our Father has strong "Paternal feelings"
too, and is also equipping you as a father for your growing family.

Day 167

"I will praise the name of God with song
and magnify Him with thanksgiving." Psalm 69:30

Real success is found in counting our blessings. Stop and
think of all God has done for you and your family! If your
list is short, or if you don't feel true gratitude and awe, then
perhaps you need to take time to reflect. It is easy
to lose focus with all the distractions, preoccupations, and
responsibilities swirling in your head. Take time to relax and recover
your peace with God – this is crucial. If disbelief or unforgiveness
are pulling you off track, then talk to a Priest, go to Confession,
and find little ways to bring more love into the area God has
put in your mind. God is there for you! He is a Living God!

"It is Jesus that you seek when you dream of happiness; He is
waiting for you when nothing else you find satisfies you; He is
the beauty to which you are so attracted; it is He who provoked
you with that thirst for fullness that will not let you settle for
compromise; it is He who urges you to shed the masks of a false
life; it is He who reads in your heart your most genuine choices,
the choices that others try to stifle." Pope Saint John Paul II

Day 168

"It is better to take refuge in the Lord
Than to trust in man. The Lord has helped me.
The Lord is my strength and song,
and He has become my salvation." Psalm 118:8, 14

We are all influenced by our surroundings: the media, latest
trends, and the customs of our time. However, the "Quality of
Life" we seek, cannot be found in and through man and our
society. True peace, love, and joy can only come from Above.
Therefore, let your heart be guided by the Holy Spirit to find
your True Worth, Real Freedom, and Genuine Fulfillment.

"It is Jesus who stirs in you the desire to do something great with
your lives, the will to follow an ideal, the refusal to allow yourselves
to be ground down by mediocrity, the courage to commit yourselves
humbly and patiently to improving yourselves and society, making
the world more human and more fraternal."
Pope Saint John Paul II

Day 169

Fatherhood
"As a father has compassion on his children, so the
LORD has compassion on those who fear him." *Psalm 103:13*

"Fatherhood is a vocation in God's service, to be not held lightly
*or frivolously, but with the **serious determination***
***of serious men**." Fr. Lawrence Lovasik*

"We are not some casual and meaningless product of evolution.
Each of us is the result of a thought of God." *Pope Benedict XVI*

"When I was a boy of 14, my father was so ignorant I could hardly stand
to have the old man around. But when I got to be 21, I was astonished
at how much the old man had learned in seven years." Mark Twain

"A Father's blessing gives his family strong roots." *Sirach 3:9*

Day 170

Mary said, "My soul exalts the Lord,
and my spirit has rejoiced in God my Savior.
For He has had regard for the humble state
of His handmaid." *Luke 1:46-48a*

The Feminine Element
"The hour is coming, in fact has come, when the vocation of women is
being acknowledged in its fullness, the hour in which women acquire in
the world an influence, an effect and a power never hitherto achieved.
That is why, at this moment when the human race is undergoing so
*deep a transformation, **women imbued with a spirit of the gospel***
***can do so much to aid humanity in not falling**."*
Closing message of the Second Vatican Council

"It is theologically and anthropologically important for woman to be
at the center of Christianity. Through Mary, and the other holy women,
the feminine element stands at the heart of the Christian religion."
Pope Benedict XVI

Day 171

"May the God of hope fill you with all joy and peace in believing, so that you will abound in hope by the power of the Holy Spirit." Romans 15:13

Always persevere with Christ in Hope beyond Hope!
You can run the race with His grace!
He transforms and fuels our hearts so we can deliver our best.

"Faith is what gets you started.
Hope is what keeps you going.
Love is what brings you to the end."
Mother Angelica, EWTN

"We exult in hope of the glory of God. And not only this, but we also exult in our tribulations, knowing that tribulation brings about perseverance; and perseverance, proven character; and proven character, hope; and hope does not disappoint, because the love of God has been poured out within our hearts through the Holy Spirit who was given to us." Romans 5:2b-5

Day 172

*"I will put enmity between you and the woman,
and between your seed and her seed; He shall bruise you on the head,
and you shall bruise him on the heel." Genesis 3:15*

"Mary - the "woman" of the Bible (*Gen.* 3:15) - intimately belongs
to the salvific mystery of Christ, and is therefore also present in a special
way in the mystery of the Church. Since "the Church is in Christ
as a sacrament... of intimate union with God and of the unity of the
whole human race", the special presence of the Mother of God in
the mystery of the Church makes us think *of the exceptional link
between this "woman" and the whole human family."*
"It is significant that Saint Paul does not call the **Mother of Christ**
by her own name "Mary", but calls her "woman": this coincides
with the words of the Proto-evangelium in the Book of Genesis (cf.
3:15). She is that "woman" who is present in the central salvific
event which marks the "fullness of time": this event is realized in her
and through her." Pope St. John Paul II, *"Mulieris Dignitatem"*
**"When the time had fully come, God sent forth
His Son, born of a woman".** *Galatians 4:4*

Day 173

"The Word is truly made flesh" John 1:14

"Do we not find in the Annunciation at Nazareth the beginning of that definitive answer by which *God himself "attempts to calm people's hearts"?* It is not just a matter here of God's words revealed through the Prophets; rather with this response "the Word is truly made flesh" (cf. *Jn* 1:14). Hence *Mary* attains *a union with God that exceeds* all the expectations of the human spirit." Pope St. John Paul II, *Mulieris Dignitatem*

"When the woman works within her natural, receptive nature, she is personally fulfilled and the community around her is blessed by the feminine aspect of the human experience. *When women are open to receiving life, **the world flowers once again**. Receptivity is the foundation of all other feminine attributes. The woman finds in each life something **unrepeatable, something wondrous**. The gift of self for the woman is a gift of life for all of mankind.* When women work in concert with the principle of *receptivity*, they encourage pro-life and pro-family policies in the workplace and in the culture." *Mary Jo Anderson*

Day 174

"For You are my hope; O Lord God,
You are my confidence from my youth.
By You I have been sustained from my birth;
You are He who took me from my mother's womb;
My praise is continually of You." Psalm 71:5-6

It is the Lord who sustains us from our mother's womb!
He is there from the beginning, throughout our life, and on - until He
calls us Home to eternal life. He always provides and is faithful. How
can we question Our Creator's love and support? He is always true!
Could we be loved anymore; has anyone sacrificed more for our good?

"Know therefore that the Lord your God, He is God,
the faithful God, who keeps His covenant and His loving
kindness to a thousandth generation with those who love Him
and keep His commandments." Deuteronomy 7:9

Day 175

"It shall come about, because you listen to these judgments and keep
and do them, that the Lord your God will keep with you His covenant
and His loving kindness which He swore to your forefathers. He will
love you and bless you and multiply you; He will also bless the fruit
of your womb and the fruit of your ground." Deuteronomy 7:12-13a

Our Lord blesses us and rewards our loyalty to Him. He only asks that we
keep a 'healthy' relationship with Him. To do so, we must take the time to
know Him. This is not a burden on our time. At times we may be tempted
not act, or to put it off for tomorrow. However, once we take the first step,
this new daily habit will overwhelms us in a new dimension. Our heart
changes and grows; then suddenly we truly desire to please & serve God.
Dear Holy Spirit please bless me with the:
Spirit of Knowledge - that I may know God and His plan for my life;
Spirit of Piety - that I *may find time* to *be of service* to God;
and *Spirit of Fear* - that I may be filled with a loving reverence
towards God, and thus give my all to follow and please Him.

Day 176

*"For thus says the high and exalted One, who lives forever,
whose name is Holy, 'I dwell on a high and holy place, and also
with the contrite and lowly of spirit; In order to revive the spirit
of the lowly and to revive the heart of the contrite."* Isaiah 57:15

*As we grow in our spirit, we will feel gratitude to the Holy & Exalted One
for giving us life, and for patiently waiting on us to recognize His gifts.
Although we can be 'too busy' with life, Our Lord doesn't give up on
us. Instead, He still chooses to give generously even when our faith is
lacking or our love vacillates; and even when we only remember Him
for what we need. Our Lord still persists in His noble & willing heart
always ready to forgive us. He patiently waits for us to call upon Him,
and when we do finally remember Him, He is so merciful and gracious
in return. His forgiveness is the greatest gift; yet He still blesses us
again by renewing our spirit, so that we can soar to new heights of
love & joy in our life. He wants our faith & happiness to grow!*

*"Truly I say to you, if you have faith the size of a mustard seed,
you will say to this mountain, 'Move from here to there,' and it
will move; and nothing will be impossible to you."* Matthew 17:20

Day 177

"The earth is the LORD's, and all it contains,
The world, and those who dwell in it. Psalm 24:1

"His Will called us out of nothingness." Our Lord has created all with
His mighty hands. Prior to God's love for us – nothing existed – nada.
This all powerful God is the same God that holds you and your baby,
so gently in the palm of His hands.

"The Hand that formed each of us left Its imprint upon
our minds and souls for He made us to His own image.
The soul He breathed into this work of His Hands - our body -
was imprinted with His love - His creative power - His strength.
We reflect His eternity, for once His Will called us out of
nothingness, we became immortal—our soul will never die.
God has our entire lives in the palm of His loving Hands - we can
rest secure about our past, present and future for He loves us."
Mother M. Angelica, EWTN

Day 178

*"**In the beginning God created the heavens and the earth.**" Genesis 1:1*

Many Scientists and Researches spend years trying to figure out how life began. Some still think they may find some obscure element they may have missed. However, God creates as He wills "out of nothing", (Lateran Council IV, 1215). Our Creator's wisdom is beyond our comprehension. It is He who created our universe with over one hundred billion galaxies, one being our own Milky Way Galaxy that has a minimum of 100 billion planets. Yet this noble Creator's greatest masterpiece is you and your developing child. We are made by the same Creator that established our universe!

"*Nothing is nothing*, and from nothing, nothing comes, since nothing is... nothing!" So how did the universe come into existence? The reality of our universe "demands the existence of a singularity and therefore, of a Creator outside space and time."
"This theory has become so scientifically solid, that 50% of astrophysicists are accepting a metaphysical conclusion: ***The need of a Creator.***"
"Spontaneous creation is the reason there is something rather than nothing, why the Universe exists, why we exist." Fr. Robert J. Spitzer, S.J, PhD

Day 179

"The steadfast of mind You will keep in perfect peace,
Because he trusts in You." Isaiah 26:3

"Blessed are the poor in spirit, for theirs is the Kingdom of Heaven.
"Blessed are those who mourn, for they shall be comforted.
"Blessed are the gentle, for they shall inherit the earth.
"Blessed are those who hunger and thirst for
righteousness, for they shall be satisfied.
"Blessed are the merciful, for they shall receive mercy.
"Blessed are the pure in heart, for they shall see God.
"Blessed are the peacemakers, for they shall be called sons of God.
"Blessed are those who have been persecuted for the sake
of righteousness, for theirs is the Kingdom of Heaven.
"Blessed are you when people insult you and persecute you,
and falsely say all kinds of evil against you because of Me.
Rejoice and be glad, for your reward in Heaven is great; for in the same
way they persecuted the prophets who were before you." Matthew 5:3-12

Day 180

"So give Your servant an understanding heart to judge Your people to discern between good and evil." 1 Kings 3:9a

Ask God to help you grow in discernment –
an important gift to judge well.

"Lord, make me an instrument of Your peace.
Where there is hatred, let me sow love;
Where there is injury, pardon; where there is doubt, faith;
Where there is despair, hope; where there is darkness, light;
Where there is sadness, joy.
O, Divine Master, grant that I may not so much seek to be consoled as to
console; to be understood as to understand; to be loved as to love; For it
is in giving that we receive; it is in pardoning that we are pardoned; it is
in dying that we are born again to eternal life." Saint Francis of Assisi

Day 181

"While Jesus was saying these things, one of the women in the crowd raised her voice and said to Him, 'Blessed is the womb that bore You and the breasts at which You nursed." Luke 11:27

Consider nursing your baby. The American Academy of Pediatrics recommends breastfeeding for the first six months (at least) since breast milk has many benefits for your little one. Breast milk contains vitamins, nutrients and disease-fighting substances that protect your baby from illness. This antibody is called Immunoglobulin A and is present in the colostrum - the first milk your body produces for your baby. It guards against invading germs to give your baby a kick-start in developing His/her own immune system. It can also help protect your baby from developing allergies.

"And you will be nursed, you will be carried on the hip and fondled on the knees." Isaiah 66:12

Day 182

"Rejoice in hope, persevere in tribulation, be devoted to prayer." Romans 12:12

"It is good for us at times to have troubles and adversities, for often they make a man enter into himself, so that he may know that he is in exile, and may not place his hopes on anything in this world. For then do we the more seek God for our inward witness, when outwardly we are slighted by men and incur discredit. Therefore ought a man to establish himself so firmly in God that he has no need to seek many human consolations."
Thomas à Kempis

"Never forget that there are only two philosophies to rule your life: The one of the cross, which starts with the fast and ends with the feast. The other of Satan, which starts with the feast and ends with the headache."
Fulton J. Sheen, "Seven Words of Jesus and Mary"

Day 183

"Therefore I say to you, whatever you ask in prayer, believe that you have received it, and it will be granted to you." *Mark 11:24*

Do you remember when you were young that you may have hoped for a particular gift at Christmas time? Perhaps you received it, or perhaps you had to wait another year or two. Some parents just can't afford to buy "another" toy, or the "Big Expensive" one. Perhaps your parents were being careful not to over indulge their children. Now as an adult, you may decide to buy the same 'treasure' you had once hoped for, for your own child. Your gratification may have been delayed, but I am sure you will live the experience and the joy - even more - through your child's delight. In turn, we need to understand God's response to our prayers, even if the answer is delayed or a little different than what we originally had hoped for. God's wisdom & timing is always perfect.

"But the wisdom from above is first pure, then peaceable, gentle, open to reason, full of mercy and good fruits, impartial and sincere." *James 3:17*

Day 184

"On the day I called, You answered me; You made me bold with strength in my soul." *Psalm 138:3*

As a Mother with child, you may be wondering whether you will have the strength and the knowledge to be a strong and wise parent. Fathers may also feel overwhelmed with this new responsibility to care for *another* person. God clearly states, *"I will put My law within them and on their heart I will write it; and I will be their God, and they shall be My people"*, *(Jer. 31:33)*. God will lead you, equip you, and give you the strength in your heart and soul that you need.

Ask the Holy Spirit to make you "bold with strength in your soul".

"Arise! For it is your task and responsibility, but we will be with you; be courageous and do it." *Ezra 10:4*

"Moreover, I will give you a new heart and put a new spirit within you; and I will remove the heart of stone from your flesh and give you a heart of flesh." *Ezekiel 36:26*

Day 185

Therefore if anyone is in Christ, he is a new creation; the old things passed away; behold, new things have come. *2 Corinthians 5:17*

"The aim of all Christian education, moreover, is to train the believer in an adult faith that can make him a "new creation", capable of bearing witness in his surroundings to the Christian hope that inspires him."
Pope Benedict XVI, *The Sacrament Of Charity*

"Once you have surrendered yourself, you make yourself receptive. In receiving from God, you are perfected and completed."
Fulton J. Sheen, *Seven Words of Jesus and Mary: Lessons from Cana & Calvary*

"Whatever you do, do your work heartily, as for the Lord rather than for men." *Colossians 3:23*

Everything we do is a choice; whether we act, react, or don't act at all. We must choose to either follow God's ways or the world's ways. Be receptive to God's leading!

Day 186

"May integrity and honesty be their virtue
and their protection." Psalm 25:21

Parents must create a home where integrity and honesty are key.
Our children pick up on every detail of what we say and what we
do (or don't do). So as Parents, we must give our best example
to our children. Try to study the virtues and ask God to help you
grow in them. Then you will be strengthened with the knowledge
and wisdom to lead your little one, who will be looking up to you
for direction. Also, be patient with them as they grow. Our world
projects so much confusion. It takes time and the proper education
to direct or redirect them, until they truly understand God's
truths. Remember, to be patient with yourself too, as you grow
and develop in character and virtues. It takes time for all of us!

This says it all: **Please be patient with me, God isn't finished with me yet.**

'Fathers, do not provoke your children to anger, but bring them
up in the discipline and instruction of the Lord.' Eph. 6:4

Third Trimester

Almost There! You probably can't wait to see your Baby!
Your baby's lungs are not fully mature yet, but some rhythmic
breathing movements are occurring. His/her bones are
fully developed now, but are still soft and pliable.

Seventh Month
(28-32 weeks)

Now your baby measures about twelve to sixteen inches in length, and
weighs approximately four pounds. Due to your baby's increased size,
he/she will begin to take a more typical fetal position, where the legs are
bent up towards the chest. Also during this month, your baby's eyelids
will begin to open, and taste buds will begin to develop. Now your baby
is ablr to experience four senses: vision, hearing, touch and taste. As
the baby grows larger, you may be experiencing more pressure on your
stomach and bladder. You may also notice slight swelling in your ankles.
Try to lie down or prop your feet up as much as possible. Get plenty of
rest and eat well balanced meals. You both need good nourishment!

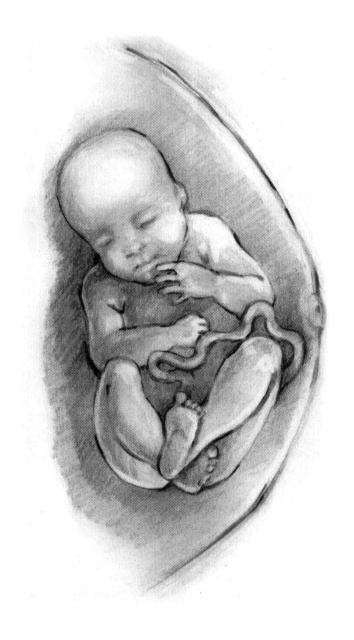

Day 187

*"Behold, an angel of the Lord appeared to Joseph in a
dream and said, 'Arise and take the Child and his Mother,
and flee to Egypt. Remain there until I tell you, for
Herod is going to search for the Child to kill Him.'
So he arose and took the Child and His Mother during
the night and departed for Egypt.'"* Matthew 2:13-14

*Have you ever really thought about the depth of Mary and Joseph's YES
to God? Her pregnancy was at first very upsetting to Joseph, since she
was found to be with Child during their betrothal. Mary could have
been stoned for this, but Joseph was enlightened in a dream to know
that this Child was conceived through the power of the Holy Spirit.
Then later in the third trimester, at full term, she rides on a donkey
to Bethlehem to be registered - bouncing up & down on a donkey for
miles! Can you also imagine, not knowing where you would be giving
birth? They end up in a poor, dirty stable - since there is no room
for Our Lord! No medical help either. And as soon as Jesus is born,
they have to leave for Egypt, in fear that Baby Jesus will be killed by
Herod's soldiers - who did kill hundreds of babies in the Massacre
of Innocents! Can you imagine taking off so quickly after birth, not
knowing where or how you will care for This Precious Little One?*
**What fortitude and faith The Holy Family showed.
What a Leap of Faith & Trust in God's Provision!**

Day 188

"The LORD's loving kindness is from everlasting to everlasting
with those who fear Him (are in awe of Him),
and His righteousness is with their children's children." Psalm 103:17

Ask God to help you direct your children towards God's excellence.
"To live well is nothing other than to love God with all one's heart, with
all one's soul and with all one's efforts; from this it comes about that
love is kept whole and uncorrupted (by temperance). No misfortune
can disturb it (with fortitude). It obeys only God (which is justice), and
is careful in discerning things, so as not to be surprised by deceit or
trickery (which is prudence)," St. Augustine, De Moribus Eccl.

"As those first responsible for the education of their children,
parents have the right to choose a school for them which corresponds
to their own convictions. This right is fundamental. As far as possible
parents have the duty of choosing schools that will best help them in their
task as Christian educators." CCC 2229

Day 189

"I slept, but my heart was vigilant." Song 5:2

"Are there more important "facts" to know about a man? The love of his heart, the work of his hands—that's all we really need to know. *You can tell a man's character by the love of his life and the work of his hands.* The woman he chooses to love and to marry and to stay with for life; the quality of his work, however humble and hidden it might be. That is what makes a man a man. But what makes a man not only good, but a Saint, is how he responds to God. Nature drives a man to work and to marry. Grace moves him to make of marriage and work an offering acceptable to God. *When you commit yourself to seeking God in all things, then all things can become the means to holiness.* Grace enables us to see God working in places where we thought only man should go: the workshop, the home, the roads on which we travel. We know that St Joseph saw the hand of God clearly in all of these places because he served God so faithfully and silently in them. That openness to God shows forth in the way a man loves and works. *He is not living for himself,* to make a name for himself, to lay hold of fame and fortune. He works and loves in a prayerful spirit, so that he can be prompt to obey when God calls him to act in a special way." *Fr. John Henry Hanson, O. Praem*

Day 190

"Oh give thanks to the LORD, call upon His name;
Make known His deeds among the peoples. Remember
His covenant forever, the word which He commanded
to a thousand generations." I Chronicles 16:8, 15

Saint Joseph is known as the Patron of the Universal Church,
for his faithfulness, trust, and obedience to God's inspirations!

"There are many good reasons to honor Saint Joseph, and to learn
from his life. He was a man of strong faith. He earned a living
for his family — Jesus and Mary — with his own hard work ...
He guarded the purity of the Blessed Virgin, who was his Spouse.
And he respected — he loved!
In God's freedom, when God made his choice:
not only his choice of Our Lady the Virgin as his Mother, but
also his choice of Saint Joseph as the Husband of Holy Mary."
St. Josemaria Escriva

Day 191

"When my anxious thoughts multiply within me,
Your consolations delight my soul." Psalm 94:19

Don't be overwhelmed or anxious about the upcoming birth of your child.
It is natural to wonder what it will be like when the time comes to give
birth. We hope and pray for a healthy delivery for your baby and Mom.
Ask the Lord to comfort you with His peace. He will be there for both of
you on that special day. Throughout the Bible there are countless stories
and promises confirming just how faithful the Lord has always been to
a thousand generations. He is with us now too. He is a living God!
He is there for us: yesterday, today and tomorrow;
His Loyalty is always TRUE!

"I love You, O LORD, my strength. The LORD is my rock and my
fortress; my deliverer, My God; my rock, in whom I take refuge;
my shield and the horn of my salvation, my stronghold. I call
upon the LORD, who is worthy to be praised." Psalm 18:1-3a

Day 192

"We are no longer to be children, tossed here and there by waves and carried about by every wind of doctrine, by the trickery of men, by craftiness in deceitful scheming; but speaking the truth in love, we are to grow up in all aspects into Him who is the head, even Christ, from whom the whole body, being fitted and held together by what every joint supplies, according to the proper working of each individual part, causes the growth of the body for the building up of itself in love." Ephesians 4:14-16

We are called to be strong and courageous, so as not to be tossed about by changing fads or passing ideologies. We are not called to be of this world, nor to be "politically correct" for others (they aren't God). Many just go along with the crowd and give in to peer pressure – to be accepted by them. However, as followers of Christ, we are called to grow in unity with the Spirit, as one body under one Lord, the Father of us all. We are called to work together for the building up of the whole body. Each of us is equipped by God with special graces to be of service in edifying and encouraging one another in love.

Day 193

"The father of the righteous will greatly rejoice,
And he who begets a wise son will be filled with joy.
Let your father and your mother be glad,
And let her rejoice who gave birth to you." Proverbs 23:24-25

The glory of God blossoms in every birth. All mothers and fathers
have high hopes for their children's future. If we choose to make
Our Lord the cornerstone of our life, then His purpose and plan will
be realized, and our children will be blessed. So set your heart on
Christ. Then find a special time to pray to Him every morning and
every evening, that He may lead you and your family. God wants
us to grow with Him, to increase in knowledge and understanding.
Adoration is a special way to pray. It is a time of grace in His Presence,
when Our Lord calls us to Himself and transforms us. We should
make time to pray before Our Lord in the sacred Eucharistic Host.
As we adore and contemplate the Mystery of Christ, who is present
before us, we can listen in silence as He speaks to our hearts.

"If you knew the gift of God!" John 4:10

Day 194

"Great is the Lord and most worthy of praise;
His greatness no one can fathom." Psalm 145:3

"It may seem like you're sitting still right now, but it's an illusion of miraculous proportions. Planet Earth is spinning around its axis at an equatorial speed of 1,040 miles per hour. Simultaneously, we're also speeding through space at an average velocity of 67,108 miles per hour. That's not just faster than a speeding bullet. It's 87 times faster than the speed of sound. So even on a day when you feel like you didn't get much done, you did travel 1,599,793 miles through space! And to top things off, the Milky Way Galaxy is spinning like a top at the mind-boggling rate of 483,000 mph. If that isn't miraculous, I don't know what is. Yet when was the last time you thanked God for keeping us in orbit? I'm guessing never! "Lord, I wasn't sure we'd make the full rotation today, but You did it again!" We just don't pray that way. Why? Because God is so good at what God does that we take it for granted. Now here's my point. You already believe God for the big miracles like they're no big deal. The trick is learning to trust Him for the little ones."

Mark Batterson, *"You aren't just surrounded by miracles, you are one"*

Day 195

"He performs wonders that cannot be fathomed,
miracles that cannot be counted." Job 5:9
"Trillions of chemical reactions are taking
place in your body every second
of every day - you are inhaling oxygen, metabolizing energy, managing
equilibrium, manufacturing hormones, fighting antigens, filtering
stimuli, purifying toxins, and circulating six quarts of blood through
60,000 miles of arteries, veins, and capillaries. If the blood vessels in
your body were laid end to end, they'd circle the earth two and a half
times! Your brain has the ability to perform ten quadrillion calculations
per second using only twenty watts of power. And its storage capacity
is 2.5 petabytes. The entire print collection of the Library of Congress
is estimated to be 10 terabytes. So your brain has the capacity to
store 250 libraries of congress. If your personal genome sequence
were written out longhand, it would be a three-billion-word book. The
King James Version has 783,137 words, so your genetic code is the
equivalent of approximately four thousand Bibles. If your personal
genome sequence were an audio book, and you were read at a rate
of one double helix per second, it would take nearly a century to put
you into words! My point? You aren't just surrounded by miracles.
You are one. *What if we started living like it?*
How would it change our daily lives? How would it change the way we
treat the walking, talking miracles we live with and work with each day?"
Mark Batterson, *"You aren't just surrounded by miracles, you are one"*

Day 196

"Only give heed to yourself and keep your soul diligently, so that you do not forget the things which your eyes have seen and they do not depart from your heart all the days of your life; but make them known to your sons and your grandsons." Deuteronomy 4:9

Victory has already been attained, so have confidence in Our Lord.

*"Cultivate thoughts of confidence as long as it pleases God to give them to you; they honor God far more than contrary thoughts. The more wretched we are - the more is God honored by the confidence we have in Him. It seems to me that if your confidence were as great as it ought to be, you would not worry about what may happen to you; you would place it all in God's hands, hoping that when He wants something of you, He will let you know what it is. Hope on to the end. Pray that - my faults, however grave and frequent, **may never make me despair of His goodness**. That, in my opinion, would be the greatest evil that could befall anyone. When we can protect ourselves against that evil, there is no other which may not turn to our good and from which we cannot easily draw great advantage."*
Saint Claude de la Colombière

Day 197

"When Jesus saw His mother, and the disciple whom He loved standing nearby, He said to His mother, 'Woman, behold, your son!' Then He said to the disciple, 'Behold, your mother!' From that hour the disciple took her into his own household." John 19:26-27

Our Lord was suffering greatly as He was dying on the cross. It was extremely painful for Him to talk. Therefore anything He said in this great agony was of extreme importance. As Scripture states above, Jesus was giving His Mother Mary to His faithful disciples, that we may take her into our hearts as our spiritual mother, just as she receives us as her spiritual daughters and sons.

"We never give more honor to Jesus than when we honor his Mother, and we honor her simply and solely to honor Him all the more perfectly. We go to her only as a way leading to the goal we seek - Jesus, her Son."
Saint Louis Marie de Montfort

"O sinner, be not discouraged, but have recourse to Mary in all your necessities. Call her to your assistance, for such is the Divine Will that she should help in every kind of necessity." Saint Basil the Great

Day 198

"When he falls, he will not be hurled headlong,
Because the LORD is the One who holds his hand.
I have been young and now I am old,
Yet I have not seen the righteous forsaken
Or his descendants begging bread.
All day long he is gracious and lends,
And his descendants are a blessing. Psalm 37:24-26

At times we fall. At times we fail. At times we are in despair.
Yet, have you not noted that God pulls us back up on our feet and gives us
new strength to carry on & move forward? He never leaves us in the mud
if we call on Him! There is a "fulfillment of hope until the end," Heb. 6:11.

"There is an appointed time for everything. And there is a
time for every event under heaven - A time to tear down and
a time to build up. A time to weep and a time to laugh;
A time to mourn and a time to dance." Ecclesiastes 3: 1, 3-4

Day 199

"The LORD protects strangers;
He supports the fatherless and the widow." Psalm 146:9
The Lord is closest to you, if you carry this heavy cross. He will comfort
you in your great loss or abandonment. Call on your heavenly Father:
daily - even hourly – that He may be your foundation and support. Give
Him your burdens. Let Him direct and make a path for you & your
family. God will bring goodness to your life; there will be recompense.
"Man's steps are ordained by the LORD,
How then can man understand his way?" *Proverbs 20:24*

"Everything comes from love,
All is ordained for the salvation of man,
God does nothing without this goal in mind."
St. Catherine of Siena

Day 200

"Thou does open Thy hand,
and does satisfy the desire of every living thing." *Psalm 145:16*

When your baby cries, you will respond according to his/her needs.
Your loving response to your child - **is a reflection of God's**
love *- and His care for you when you call upon Him.*
We are made to reflect His image – an image of a true loving relationship.

God created all things "not to increase His glory,
but to show it forth and to communicate it." *St. Bonaventure*

"Creatures came into existence when the key of love
opened his hand," *St. Thomas Aquinas*

"Nothing seems tiresome or painful when you are working for a
Master who pays well; who rewards even a cup of cold water
given for love of Him." *Saint Dominic Savio*

Day 201

"If you follow My Commandments your descendants would be like the sand, and your offspring like its grains; their names would never be cut off or destroyed from My presence." Isaiah 48:19

Have you ever really stopped to ponder how many descendants may be born from your offspring? If so, it should give you a sense of awe and a deep respect for the responsibility of being and staying faithful to Our Lord. What we do and what we choose - carries forward – it affects us and our offspring. Our faithfulness is not just a testimony of our "individual love" to honor God's goodness; it is also an important factor in developing the seeds of Faith for Future Generations – for our descendants! We must be prudent in our judgments since it affects more than just ourselves. Our decisions should inspire our family.

"The prudent man looks where he is going." Proverbs 14:15b

Prudence is "right reason in action". St. Thomas Aquinas

"Ponder the fact that God has made you a gardener, to root out vice and plant virtue." St. Catherine of Siena

Day 202

Put on the Armor of God

"Finally, be strong in the Lord and in the strength of His might. Put on the *full armor of God*, so that you will be able to stand firm against the schemes of the devil. For our struggle is not against flesh and blood, but against the rulers, against the powers, against the world forces of this darkness, against the spiritual *forces* of wickedness in the heavenly *places*. Therefore, take up the full armor of God, so that you will be able to resist in the evil day, and having done everything, to *stand firm*. Stand firm therefore, HAVING GIRDED YOUR LOINS WITH **TRUTH,** AND HAVING PUT ON THE BREASTPLATE OF **RIGHTEOUSNESS,** and having shod YOUR FEET WITH THE PREPARATION OF THE GOSPEL OF **PEACE**; in addition to all, taking up the **shield of faith** with which you will be able to extinguish all the flaming arrows of the evil *one*. And take THE **HELMET OF SALVATION,** AND THE **sword of the Spirit**, which is the **word of God**. With all prayer and petition *pray at all times in the Spirit* and with this in view, be on the alert with all *perseverance and petition for all the saints*." Ephes. 6:10-18 *As a Parent, you need to be equipped in faith - to stand firm for your little one.*

Day 203

"Her children rise up and bless her;
Her husband also, and he praises her, saying:
'Many daughters have done nobly, but you excel them all.'
Charm is deceitful and beauty is vain, but a woman who fears
the Lord, she shall be praised." Proverbs 31:28-30

A woman who is devoted to the Lord is greatly blessed in her home.
Soon you will have a lifetime of enjoyable memories and traditions to
establish with your growing family. How wonderful the holidays will be
as you share the warmth of your child's hugs as he/she embraces you!

"An excellent wife, who can find?
For her worth is far above jewels.
The heart of her husband trusts in her,
and he will have no lack of gain."
"She extends her hand to the poor, and she stretches
out her hands to the needy." Proverbs 31:10-11, 20

Day 204

"Two are better than one because they have a good return for
their labor. For if either of them falls, the other one will lift up his
companion. And if one can overpower him who is alone, two can resist
him. A cord of three strands is not quickly torn apart." Eccles. 4:9-12

Pray with your spouse to your Heavenly Father.
*This creates the **cord of three strands** that is necessary to give your*
family the stable foundation you need in faith, truth, and wisdom.
Every relationship needs to grow in God's virtues and goodness.
Please let me remind you again of St. Gerard Majella, the
Patron Saint of Expectant Mothers! Pray to him to intercede for the two
of you & your baby. I personally am very grateful and devoted to him.
We prayed over our babies and Our Lord was very gracious.
Thank you St. Gerard for your prayers of intercession!

"Here the will of God is done, as God wills, and as
long as God wills." Saint Gerard Majella

Day 205

In faithfulness to God's truth, I need to also direct you to facts you need to know and understand once your little one is born:
In January, 2015, Pope Francis stated, "Be sanctuaries of respect for life, proclaiming the sacredness of every human life from conception to natural death. What a gift this would be to society if every Christian family lived fully its noble vocation." Pope Francis also reminded the faithful that Pope Paul VI "courageously" wrote the 1968 encyclical "Humanae Vitae", which explains the church's opposition to artificial birth control. Artificial birth control does not leave an "openness to life". It can also act as an abortifacient, since the Pill causes the endometrium (the lining of your womb) to become thin, so it cannot support implantation of your newly conceived child. Natural Family Planning (NFP) is a healthy alternative to artificial birth control, (NFP is not the Rhythm Method). The Couple to Couple League and all Pro-Life organizations can give you more information on this matter to help you. Please pray about this.

Day 206

"He will bring me into the light, and I will see his victory." *Micah 7:9*
"There are many injustices in our society, but the most fundamental is
the one our society rarely acknowledges - the routine taking of innocent
human life every day through abortion. The injustice of abortion includes
the millions who have been killed before they had a chance to come into
the world. Even more than that, the acceptance of abortion also sends
the signal throughout society that human life is disposable and that some
lives are not even worth protecting. Legalized abortion has also misled
our leaders into thinking they can solve problems in our society by taking
lives or preventing lives from being born. Pope Francis linked abortion,
euthanasia, and birth control to a "culture of waste" that leads us to value
human life only according to material standards. Pope Francis said:
'We discard whatever is not useful to this logic; it is this attitude that …
leads people to discard babies through abortion. The culture of waste
also leads to a hidden euthanasia of older people, who are abandoned.
That means we need to stand with all those who are suffering in our
society, beginning with those who are most innocent and vulnerable, the
unborn, and the elderly. We need to defend them against every aggression
- including the false compassion that suggests they would be better off
dead than they would be if they were alive, loved, and cared for.'"
Archbishop José H. Gomez, Jan 15, 2015

Day 207

"There is neither Jew nor Greek, there is neither slave nor free man, there is neither male nor female; for you are all one in Christ Jesus." *Gal. 3:28*

We are all one in Christ! God's Word is for all of us! Please understand that I love men and women equally – no favoritism here. However, since the Woman carries, I address her more often in the Mother with Child. Men are just as important in the Family structure! Men are also Co-operators with God in Life!

*"After the publication of my 'Introduction to the Devout Life', a critic chided me for addressing my Introduction to "Philothea." He said men did not want to read advice given to a woman. This puzzles me. Such men are not very manly. Devotion is for both sexes. Anyway, it is the aspiring soul that I call "Philothea." Gender is not involved. Still, rather than ignore my critic, I have addressed this new work to "Theotimus." I wonder, will a woman somewhere take offense? Will she refuse to read instruction given to males? Please understand that "Theotimus" is a name I coined for the human spirit that desires to deepen devotion and progress in holy love. This spirit is found **equally** in women and in men."* St. Francis de Sales, *Treatise on the Love of God*

Day 208

"The God who made the world and all things in it, since He is Lord of heaven and earth, does not dwell in temples made with hands; nor is He served by human hands, as though He needed anything, since He Himself gives to all people life and breath and all things." Acts 17:24-25

God does not need anything from us, since He created us.
What does interest Him - is our heart & to have a relationship with us.

"Through the centuries, saints and mystics have meditated on the heart of Jesus as a fount of theological insight and spiritual passion, joining their own heart to His. They have also illustrated how the heart became a spiritual domicile where one could take up residence with the Trinity or the Holy Family." Fr. Michael Morris, O.P.

*"Then the Lord God formed man of dust from the ground, and breathed into his nostrils **the breath of life**; and man became a living being." Genesis 2:7*

Day 209

"For your husband is your Maker, Whose name is the LORD of hosts; And your Redeemer is the Holy One of Israel, Who is called the God of all the earth." Isaiah 54:5 *There are many mothers today who are "single" parents. It is hard work being a good parent, let alone a single parent. Single parents feel that they have to make twice the effort to succeed as a parent. They are overwhelmed with the "double" load they bear in being responsible for their children. Please remember that single parents said "YES" to God and to Life! They could have made another choice. Please support these courageous women and all their sacrifices. Don't judge and condemn them. How can people weigh one sin over another? My sin is less & yours is more. Remember, we all fall short and God forgives us all. He is the One that remakes us – it is not from our "merits". Let's get back to a humble teaching: don't worry about 'removing the speck' from your brother's or sister's eye. They are already overwhelmed with shame. Don't we all need the gift of grace and healing from the Sacrament of Confession? Only the Lord knows and sees our hearts. Please encourage men & women to be responsible in following God's design. Please support single parents. Please pray for a "Culture of Life"!*

Day 210

His mother said to the servants,
"Do whatever He tells you to do." John 2:5

Look at Our Lady's great faith. She is asking the servants to
Do whatever Jesus asks *of them. Although Jesus reminds her that it is*
not yet His time to enter into His Ministry, their loving Mother-Son
relationship wins out. They both have enormous heart to serve!
Mary, Our Mother, is also asking us to listen to her Son!
She's asking us to - **Do whatever Our Lord asks of us.**
This is a very important teaching, especially coming from
Our Lady, who is very humble and says very little throughout Scripture.
So these words are very powerful. Also note that Mary's actions always
follow her strong faith in God. Through obedience she walks faithfully
in love and loyalty to the Holy Trinity. Mary's faith never wavered, not
even at the cross. Therefore, she should be the one to direct us to follow
her Son. Our Mother always encourages us - her children - to love and
follow God's holy will. Her hope is that we will all join the Holy Family
in Heaven. Can you imagine a Family gathering with her and her Son?

Day 211

"The angel said to her: 'Hail, full of grace, the Lord is with thee; blessed art thou among women.'" Luke 1:28

Mary untying knots goes back to the second century. St. Irenaeus of Lyons wrote, "the knot of Eve's disobedience was loosed by the obedience of Mary. For what the virgin Eve had bound fast through unbelief, this did the Virgin Mary set free through faith," (*Adversus haereses,* 3, 22). This is one of the earliest examples of describing Mary as the *"New Eve."* **Prayer to Our Lady Undoer of Knots: "Dearest Holy Mother, you are generous with all who seek you, have mercy on me. I entrust into your hands this knot which robs the peace of my heart, paralyzes my soul, and keeps me from going to my Lord and serving Him with my life. Please undo this knot in my love...., O Mother, ask Jesus to heal my paralytic faith which gets down hearted with the stones on the road. Dearest Mother, may I see these stones as friends. Not murmuring against them anymore but giving endless thanks for them, may I smile trustingly in your power and intercession." O Mary, please pray for me.**

Day 212

"For even the Son of Man did not come to be served, but to serve, and to give His life as a ransom for many." Mark 10:45

"We too are called to give our lives for our brothers and sisters, and thus to realize in the fullness of truth, the meaning and destiny of our existence." Pope Saint John Paul II

"Here I am reminded of the question of the Roman procurator Pontius Pilate, when Jesus reveals the profound meaning of his mission: **"What is truth?"** *(Jn 18: 37, 38). Pilate does not understand that "the" Truth is in front of him, he cannot see in Jesus the face of the truth, which is the face of God - yet, Jesus is just that: the Truth, which, in the fullness of time, "became flesh" (Jn 1:14), came among us so that we may know it. You cannot grab the truth as if it were an object, you encounter it. It is not a possession; it* **is an encounter with a Person***." Pope Francis*

Day 213

"When the Spirit of truth comes, 'He will guide you to all truth.'"
John 16:13
"Dear brothers and sisters, good day! Today I want to
focus on the action that the Holy Spirit accomplishes
in guiding the Church and each one of us
to the Truth. Jesus says to his disciples: the Holy Spirit, "He will guide you
to all truth" (Jn 16:13), He himself being "the Spirit of truth" (cf. Jn
14:17; 15:26; 16:13). We live in an age that is rather skeptical of truth.
Benedict XVI has spoken many times of relativism, that is,
the tendency to believe that nothing is definitive, and to
think that the truth is given by consent or by what we want.
The question arises: does "the" truth really exist?
What is "the" truth? Can we know it? Can we find it?
Who helps us recognize that Jesus is "the" Word of Truth, the only
begotten Son of God the Father? St. Paul teaches that "no one can say,
"Jesus is Lord," except by the Holy Spirit" (1 Cor 12:3). It
is the Holy Spirit, the gift of the Risen Christ, that helps us
recognize the Truth. Jesus calls Him the "Paraclete", meaning
"the One who comes to our aid," who is by our side to support
us in this journey of knowledge, and at the Last Supper,
Jesus assures his disciples that the Holy Spirit will teach them all
things, reminding them of His words (cf. Jn 14:26)." Pope Francis

Day 214

"Thy word is a lamp to my feet and a light to my path." Psalm 119:105

"What is then the *action of the Holy Spirit in our lives* and in the life of the Church, to guide us to the truth? *First of all, to remind and imprint on the hearts of believers the words that Jesus said*, and precisely through these words, *God's law* - as the prophets of the Old Testament had announced - *is inscribed in our hearts and becomes within us a principle of evaluation in our choices and of guidance in our daily actions*, it becomes *a principle of life*. Ezekiel's great prophecy is realized: "I will sprinkle clean water over you to make you clean; from all your impurities and from all your idols I will cleanse you. *I will give you a new heart, and a new spirit I will put within you. ...I will put my spirit within you so that you walk in my statutes, observe my ordinances, and keep them,"* (Eze.36:25-27). Indeed, our actions are born from deep within: *It is the heart that needs to be converted to God, and the Holy Spirit transforms it if we open ourselves to Him."* Pope Francis

Day 215

*"For where two or three have gathered together in My name,
I am there in their midst."* Matthew 18:20
*Just as your baby goes everywhere you go, likewise,
the Holy Spirit is there with you & your baby (there's two of you!).
Pregnancy is two or more gathered in His name!*

*"O my God, Trinity whom I adore, help me forget myself
entirely so as to establish myself in you, unmovable
and peaceful as if my soul were already
in eternity. May nothing be able to trouble
my peace or make me leave you,
O my unchanging God, may each minute bring me more deeply
into your mystery! Grant my soul peace. Make it your heaven,
your beloved dwelling and the place of your rest. May I never
abandon you there, but may I be there, whole and entire, completely
vigilant in my faith, entirely adoring, and wholly given over
to your creative action." Blessed Elizabeth of the Trinity*

**Jesus said, "If anyone loves Me, he will keep My word;
and My Father will love him, and We will come to
him and make Our abode with him."** *Jn 14:23*

Day 216

"Ask, and it will be given to you; seek, and you will find;
knock, and it will be opened to you. For everyone who asks receives,
and he who seeks finds, and to him who knocks
It will be opened." Matthew 7:7-8

Be encouraged to ask, seek, and knock,
for the Lord is politely waiting to hear from each of us.
Yes, politely – since He awaits and needs to be invited into our hearts,
in consideration of the fact that He always respects our free will.
Jesus is always moved by Divine love and the immense mercy
in His heart. That is why we call Him: The Sacred Heart.
Call on Him with a contrite heart. He wants to hear from all of us.
The only difference between St. Peter and Judas, as
to their denial & betrayal of Christ, is that St Peter
sought out Our Lord's mercy and forgiveness.
The other gave up in despair and didn't trust Our Lord's Sacred Heart.

"I love those who love me;
and those who diligently seek me will find me." Proverbs 8:17
"Whatever you ask in prayer, believe that you have received it,
and it will be yours." Mark 11:24

Day 217

"What man is there among you who, when his son asks for a loaf, will give him a stone? If you then, being evil, know how to give good gifts to your children, how much more will your Father who is in heaven give what is good to those who ask Him!" Matthew 7:9, 11

The love that overflows in our hearts for our children is heartwarming; yet, it is only a flicker compared to the great fire of love God has in His heart for us!

"The dignity of man rests above all on the fact that he is called to communion with God. This invitation to converse with God is addressed to man as soon as he comes into being. For if man exists it is because God has created him through love, and through love continues to hold him in existence. He cannot live fully according to truth unless he freely acknowledges that love and entrusts himself to his Creator."
Vatican Council II, GS 19 § 1

Eighth Month
(33-36 weeks)

By now you are quite aware of your baby's movements. These movements will be strong enough to be visible from the outside. In fact, many mother's and father's look forward to this daily dialogue of their baby's kicking! The baby is almost fully developed this month. He/she may weigh about 5 pounds, and may measure about 17 inches in length from head to toe. All along, your baby has been acquiring immunity to infection via your antibodies, that pass through the placenta into the baby's bloodstream. This immunity will last for a few months after birth, as the baby begins to develop his/her own resistance to illness. Your baby also absorbs a gallon of amniotic fluid per day. Every three hours this fluid is completely replaced. You may be feeling more pressure on your bladder as the month progresses, since the baby's head will begin to settle down in the pelvic cavity. Hopefully you have started your childbirth classes. This is always a good idea to learn breathing techniques, to share experiences, and to speak to others who can answer your questions.

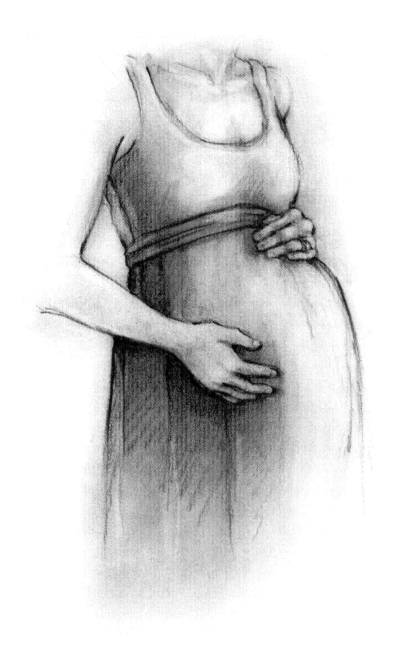

Day 218

"Did You not clothe me with skin and flesh,
and knit me together with bones and sinews?
You have granted me life and loving kindness;
and Your care has preserved my spirit." Job 10:11-12

The Lord has never fashioned another human being who is just like you,
nor like your baby. You are both uniquely special in the whole
universe, and throughout all time. God's love for each of you is
more then you could ever imagine.

"As each one has received a special gift, employ it in serving one
another as good stewards of the manifold grace of God." 1 Peter 4:10

"God saw all that He had made, and behold,
it was very good." Genesis 1:31

Day 219

Jesus spoke another parable to them, "The kingdom of heaven is like
yeast which leavens the whole measure of dough." Matthew 13:33

"What is urgently called for is a general mobilization of consciences and
a united ethical effort to activate a great campaign in support of life.
*All together, **we must build a new culture of life**...The purpose of the*
Gospel, in fact, is "to transform humanity from within and to make
it new". Like the yeast which leavens the whole measure of dough (cf.
Mt 13:33), the Gospel is meant to permeate all cultures and give
them life from within, so that they may express the full truth about
the human person and about human life. The first and fundamental
*step towards this cultural **transformation consists in forming***
consciences with regard to the incomparable and inviolable
***worth of every human life**. It is the greatest importance to re-*
establish the essential connection between life and freedom... No
less critical in the formation of conscience is the recovery of the
necessary link between freedom and truth." Pope Saint John Paul II

Day 220

"Your descendants will also be like the dust of the earth, and you will spread out to the west and to the east and to the north and to the south; and in you and in your descendants shall all the families of the earth be blessed." Genesis 28:14

"At the dawn of salvation, it is the *Birth of a Child* which is proclaimed as joyful news: "I bring you good news of a great joy which will come to all the people; for to you is born this day in the city of David a Savior, who is Christ the Lord" (Lk 2:10-11). The source of this "great joy" is the Birth of the Savior; but Christmas also reveals the *full meaning of every human birth*, and the joy which accompanies the Birth of the Messiah is thus seen to be the foundation and fulfillment of *joy at every child born* into the world (cf. Jn 16:21)." ***Pope Saint John Paul II, EVANGELIUM VITAE***

Consider the blessings that will flow from your life, the life of your children, and generations to come. May the Lord's grace & joy bless all of your future descendants. O, the joy of every birth, what incredible blessings!

Day 221

*"Many, O L*ᴏʀᴅ *my God, are the wonders which You have done,*
And Your thoughts toward us; there is none to compare with You.
If I would declare and speak of them, they would be
too numerous to count." Psalm 40:5

Who can fathom or rival the enormity of God's generous love for us?
Only God – inspires our soul. Only God - is
truly admirable beyond measure.

"Everything God created is good and His Goodness is so diffusive
that the quantities, qualities and dimensions of His creation stagger
the mind. The variety of fruit, each with its own taste, size and
color; the variety of flowers, rocks, precious stones;—everything
He created overflows in abundance. His Goodness gives me music,
friendship, love, joy, happiness, success and all the other good
things that cross my path to thrill my soul. His Goodness gives me
reflections of Himself in the intellect of man, the immensity of
the universe, the variety of creatures and the beauty
of the earth." Mother M. Angelica, EWTN

Day 222

*"As for you, speak the things which are fitting for sound doctrine.
Older men are to be temperate, dignified, sensible, sound in faith,
in love, and in perseverance. Older women likewise are to be reverent
in their behavior, not malicious gossips nor enslaved to much wine,
teaching what is good, so that they may encourage the young women to
love their husbands, to love their children, to be sensible, pure, workers
at home, kind, being subject to their own husbands, so that the word
of God will not be dishonored. Likewise urge the young men
to be sensible; in all things show yourself to be an example
of good deeds, with purity in doctrine, dignified, sound
in speech which is beyond reproach." Titus 2:1-8*

**"Now for this very reason also, applying all diligence, in your faith
supply moral excellence, and in your moral excellence, knowledge, and
in your knowledge, self-control, and in your self-control, perseverance,
and in your perseverance, godliness, and in your godliness, brotherly
kindness, and in your brotherly kindness, love."** *2 Peter 1:5-7*

Day 223

*"God will supply all your needs according to His riches
in the glory of Christ Jesus." Philippians 4:19*

Prayer for a Safe Delivery

*"O great Saint Gerard, beloved servant of Jesus Christ, perfect imitator
of your meek and humble Savior, and devoted child of the Mother of
God, enkindle within my heart one spark of that heavenly fire of charity
which glowed in your heart and made you an angel of love.
O glorious Saint Gerard, because when falsely accused of crime, you
did bear, like your Divine Master, without murmur or complaint,
the calumnies of wicked men, you have been raised up by God
as the **Patron Saint &Protector of Expectant Mothers.** Please preserve
me from danger and from the excessive pains accompanying childbirth,
and shield the child which I now carry, that my baby may see the light
of day and receive the purifying and life giving waters of baptism
through Jesus Christ our Lord. Amen"*
**Time to consider and talk to your Priest concerning the
Sacrament of Baptism - Your child's entry into the Faith & the Church!**

Day 224

*"Behold, I am with you and will keep you wherever you go,
and will bring you back to this land; for I will not leave you
until I have done what I have promised you." Genesis 28:15*

*Our Lord is always there for us even when we wander off course. If
He seems silent to us, perhaps we haven't been in touch with Him for a
long time. In truth, if He didn't think of us and smile at us every day, we
wouldn't exist. He is our lifeline – He preserves us! All He asks for –
is a heart open to communicate with Him. He just wants us
to try to give our best. In time, our weaknesses will actually
become our strengths – only in and through His grace.
Remember, prayer is a heart-to-heart exchange. We are always
in His thoughts and designs; we just need to find the time
to honor Him in our thoughts and our designs as well.
**"May the Lord, the God of your fathers, increase you
a thousand-fold more than you are and bless you, just
as He has promised you!** Deuteronomy 1:11*

Day 225

"But as for me, I will watch expectantly for the Lord;
I will wait for the God of my salvation. My God will hear me.
Do not rejoice over me, O my enemy.
Though I fall I will rise; Though I dwell in darkness,
the Lord is a light for me." *Micah 7:7-8*

God is always willing to: forgive us, love us, and be a light for us. At times
*we all **Fall**, but He will **raise** us up! Follow our Lord's light & hope.*

"I will say to God my rock, 'Why have You forgotten me?
Why do I go mourning because of the oppression of the enemy?
My adversaries revile me, while they say to me all day long,
'Where is your God?'
Why are you in despair, O my soul?
And why have you become disturbed within me?
Hope in God, for I shall yet praise Him,
The help of my countenance and my God.'" *Psalm 42: 9-11*

Day 226

"Do not be conformed to this world, but be transformed by the
renewing of your mind, so that you may prove what the will of God is,
that which is good and acceptable and perfect." *Romans 12:2*

Set your goals on Eternity – envision being with the Holy Family! Prepare
for your little one's future and be equipped in God's truth, so you
can obtain this goal together!
"Brothers and sisters: If there is any encouragement in Christ,
any solace in love, any participation in the Spirit,
any compassion and mercy, complete my joy by being of the same
mind, with the same love, united in heart, intent on one purpose.
Do nothing out of selfishness or out of vainglory;
rather, humbly regard others as more important than yourselves,
each looking out not for his own interests,
but also for the interests of others." *Philippians 2:1-4*

Day 227

"O LORD, *my heart is not proud, nor my eyes haughty;*
Nor do I involve myself in great matters, or in things too difficult for me.
Surely I have composed and quieted my soul; like a weaned child
rests against his mother, my soul is like a weaned child within me...
Hope in the LORD, **from this time forth and forever.**" *Ps. 131:1-3*

"Consult not your fears but your hopes and your dreams. Think not
about your frustrations, but about your **unfulfilled potential.** *Concern*
yourself not with what you tried and failed in, but with
what it is still possible for you to do." *Pope John XXIII*

The virtue of Hope is an inspirational gift from God -
given in and through His grace. Hope keeps our heart
and mind set on Our Lord's expectations
for us, so that we can be with Him in eternal life. Hope raises us up when
we have lost that desire. Hope gets us up & out **to do** *what God inspires*
in our soul; To BUILD UP the Body of Christ – starting with YOU!
You have the potential!

Day 228

"For you have been bought with a price: therefore
Glorify God in your body." 1 Corinthians 6:20

Our body is not our own, since by faith we are members
of the Body of Christ. We belong to the Lord - He
redeemed us and He created us. As members
of the Body of Christ, we are connected to one another in faith and love.
We are one in Christ through the Holy Spirit. We are
Brothers and Sisters in Christ awaiting our journey home to Our Lord!
Since we belong to the body of Christ, we must treat our own
bodies with this great respect of honoring Our Lord; we are made
in His image. In being members of the Body of Christ, we must
also respect every other person. The Church teaches us about
the sanctity and dignity of every life: no matter how small - at the
point of conception, nor how old - when God calls us home.
Be a hero for life; a light of truth for those who don't understand YET!

"Do you not know that your bodies are members
of Christ?" 1 Corinthians 6:15

Day 229

"The Spirit Himself testifies with our spirit that we are children of God, and if children, heirs also, heirs of God and fellow heirs with Christ, if indeed we suffer with Him so that we may also be glorified with Him." Romans 8:16-17

As soon as we are baptized into the Christian Faith, we become a member of the Church, and a member of Christ's body. Therefore, we are no longer independent minded entities. This does not make us slaves or robots; God is not a tyrant. What this is - is an initiation to join the FAMILY OF GOD! Within the Church we will grow UP - hearing the Word of God; we will receive the Sacraments; and we will find the inspiration and expertise we need to be directed and re-directed on how to be faithful Christians witnessing Christ! Remember, we nailed Our Creator and Lord to the Cross! So we have a lot to learn, and a lot of growing ahead of us. Be Humble-let Our Lord and His Church lead YOU and YOUR FAMILY. Run the race to win – you only get one opportunity!
"If anyone competes as an athlete, he does not win the prize unless he competes according to the rules." *2 Timothy 2:5*

Day 230

"Because you are sons, God has sent forth the Spirit of His Son into our hearts, crying, 'Abba! Father!' Therefore you are no longer a slave, but a son; and if a son, then an heir through God." Galatians 4:5-7

God is so generous and noble that He sends "the Spirit of His Son into our hearts". This grace begins with Baptism, where we start life as new creatures - as heirs of God. Please understand this great dignity, that Our Loving Father has graciously allowed us to be partakers of His divine nature; as we become members of Christ's Body and of His Church. His Holy Spirit enters our heart at Baptism and then He begins His work to transform us. We ourselves don't and can't increase 'our goodness'. It is Our Lord who fashions His character in us. As we mature and grow, we must choose to cooperate & be willing to be continually transformed into Christ's character. All good can only be accomplished in and through the Most Holy Trinity.

"For as many as are the promises of God, in Him they are yes; therefore also through Him is our Amen to the glory of God through us. Now He who establishes us with you in Christ and anointed us is God, who also sealed us and gave us the Spirit in our hearts as a pledge." II Corinthians 1:20-22

Day 231

Jesus said, "Let the children to come to Me; do not hinder them;
for the kingdom of God belongs to such as these." Mark 10:14

Baptism is necessary to enter the kingdom of God!

Jesus clearly directs His disciples to baptize, "Go therefore and make
disciples of all the nations, baptizing them in the name of the Father and
the Son and the Holy Spirit, (Matthew 28:19). As nurturing parents we
must understand our responsibilities to lead the children God entrusted
us with, in both their spiritual and physical needs. Jesus clearly said,
"Let the children to come to Me."
They must be "reborn of water and the Spirit," (John 3:5).
In the past, the Baptismal Fonts were inscribed - stating that the little
one would be "regenerated", or given life "again". Clearly a distinction
between physical birth and spiritual birth! That is also why the Church
practices Infant Baptism. Basically, aim to start this "new life in Christ"
as soon as possible. The sooner the better, to get started on all those
blessings of grace that your little one will need in life.

Day 232

"They shall be My people, and I will be their God; and I will give them one heart and one way, that they may fear Me always, for their own good and for the good of their children after them." Jeremiah 32:38-39

Our children will learn from our actions. They are quick to learn who we really are, and where our heart really lies. So be devoted to Our Lord and set a good example for them. For a heart that reveres God will shine a bright light for the next generation to follow.

"Let everything take second place to our care of our children, our bringing them up to the discipline and instruction of the Lord. If from the beginning we teach them to love true wisdom, they will have great wealth and glory than riches can provide." St. John Chrysostom

"May the Lord give you increase, You and your children. May you be blessed of the Lord, Maker of heaven and earth." Psalm 115:14-15

Day 233

*"Only fear the Lord and serve Him in truth with all your heart;
for consider what great things He has done for you."* 1 Samuel 12:24

"In These Dark Days, the Church Needs Her Men to be Men"
"When I was growing up, my father would often exhort me to *'be a man.'* He would summon me to courage and responsibility, to discover the heroic capacity that was in me. St. Paul summoned forth a spiritual manhood with these words: *'We must all attain to the unity of faith and knowledge of the Son of God, to mature manhood, to the extent of the full stature of Christ, so that we may no longer be infants, tossed by waves and swept along by every wind of teaching arising from human trickery, from their cunning in the interests of deceitful scheming. Rather, living the truth in love, we should grow in every way into Him who is the head, Christ, (Eph 4:13)."* Msgr. Charles Pope

"You will know the truth, and the truth will make you free." John 8:32

Day 234

*"**The righteous are bold as a lion.**" Proverbs 28:1*

*"You know the temper of the times, how many there are who love to live delicately and shrink from whatever requires manhood and generosity; who, discover in them sufficient reasons for not obeying the salutary laws of the Church, thinking the burden laid upon them more than they can bear. The most violent passions have claimed a freer indulgence; the madness of opinion which knows no restraint, every day extends further; yet those whose principles are sound, through a misplaced timidity, are frightened, and have not the courage even to speak out their opinions boldly, far less to translate them into deeds; everywhere the worst examples are affecting public morals; wicked societies, skilled in all evil arts, are doing their best to lead the people astray, and as far as they are able, to withdraw them from God, their duty, and Christianity . . . Therefore those who speak to the people should state clearly that not only according to the law of the Gospel, but even to the **dictates of natural reason**, a man is bound to govern himself and keep his passions under strict control, and moreover, that sin cannot be expiated except by penance . . . In order therefore that Our teaching may sink into men's minds, and know what is great, to actually govern their daily lives, an attempt must be made to bring them to think and act like Christians, not less so in public than in private." Pope Leo XIII, year 1885*

Day 235

"Do not let your passions be your guide,
but keep your desires in check." Sirach 18:30

We need to be 'amazed' and 'set on fire' through our love for God.
He should focus on transforming our life first. If our hearts and
our 'intellect' are set on the world's fads and our culture's
interpretation of truth - then we will get lost. Once confusion sets in,
our conscience will be numbed by the fog that sets in. Our
conscience is designed to help us discern what is good and to
help us avoid evil. It helps us to choose the right path, because
it acts as our moral compass which leads us to Truth.

"Return to your conscience . . . Turn inward, brethren, and in
everything you do, see God as your witness." St. Augustine

"These things I have spoken to you, so that in Me you may have
peace. In the world you have tribulation, but take courage;
I have overcome the world." *John 16:33*

Day 236

*"Living the truth in love, we should grow in
every way into Christ."* Eph 4:13

"It has often been observed that men are rather disengaged from
the practice of the faith and attendance at the Sacred Liturgy.
Frankly, *There is a reason*—not a politically correct one, but a
reason nonetheless. Most of the men I talk to find the Church rather
feminized. There is much talk in the Church about forgiveness and
love, about receptivity and about being "nicer." These are fine
virtues, all of them necessary. But men also want to be engaged,
to be sent into battle, to go forth and make a difference.
After years of radical feminism, men are shamed for seeking to take
up leadership and authority in their families and in the Church. It
starts early. Any normal boy is full of spit and vinegar, is aggressive,
competitive, and anxious to test his wings. But many boys are
scolded, punished, and even *medicated* for these normal tendencies.
They are told to behave more like girls and to learn to be nicer and
to get along, etc. It will be granted that limits are necessary, but
the tendency for boys to roughhouse is normal. The scolding and
"socializing" to more feminine traits continues into early adulthood.
And then there are other cultural phenomena such as the slew of
'Men are stupid' commercials, etc." *Msgr. Charles Pope*

Day 237

"The goal of our instruction is love from a pure heart and
a good conscience and a sincere faith." 1 Timothy 5

"In children we have a great charge committed to us.
Let us bestow great care in guiding our children, to do everything so that
the Evil One may not rob us of them. But now our practice is the reverse
of this. We take all care indeed to have our farm in good order, and to
commit it to a faithful manager, we look out for the workers of the field
and the bailiff, and a clever accountant. But we do not look out for what
is much more important, for a person to whom we may commit our son
as the guardian of his morals, though this is a possession much more
valuable than all others. It is for him indeed that we take such care of
our estate. **We take care of our possessions for our children, but**
of the children themselves we take no care at all.
Form the soul of your son aright, and all the rest
will be added hereafter." *St. John Chrysostom*

Day 238

*"When I consider Your heavens, the work of Your fingers,
the moon and the stars, which You have ordained;
What is man that You take thought of him, and the son of man
that You care for him? Yet You have made him a little lower than God,
and You crown him with glory and majesty! You make him to rule over
the works of Your hands; You have put all
things under his feet."* Ps. 8:3-6

God must see great worth in us, to create such wonders for us!
What tender love and intricate preparation was performed through
the work of God's hands for our benefit. Our Lord chose to create the
majestic universe and our earth for us! All was accomplished through
His will & Sacred Heart. We came into being through an act of God
- not matter what the circumstances were politically, culturally, or
even with our parents. This act of love from God cannot be diminished
or superseded by anyone or anything. You are God's wonder and so
is your child. Even your fingerprints prove this. In all of recorded
time, with billions of people, not two fingerprints are alike. Each one
of us are uniquely imprinted; each of us have our own soul, given to
us by God. Keep this focus, that God knows your precious worth.
He willed you into Being! He willed your Baby into Being!

Day 239

"He gives strength to the weary and to him who lacks might
He increases power. Though youths grow weary and tired,
and vigorous young men stumble badly,
Yet those who wait for the LORD will gain new strength;
They will mount up with wings like eagles, they will run
And not get tired, they will walk and not become weary." Isaiah 40:29-31

During the last trimester, there may be times when you will experience surges of energy as you make your final preparations for the baby. There may also be times when you feel weary, awkward, and depleted due to your increased size and perhaps a lack of sleep. Call upon the Lord with all your needs. He will comfort you and give you the strength to carry on.

"Now Jabez called on the God of Israel, saying, "Oh that You would bless me indeed and enlarge my border, and that Your hand might be with me, and that You would keep me from harm that it may not pain me!" And God granted him what he requested." 1 Chronicles 4:10

Day 240

*"Honor your father and your mother, that your days may be prolonged in the land which the L*ORD *your God gives you." Exodus 20:12*

"For the Lord honored the father above the children, and he confirmed the right of the mother over her sons. Whoever honors his father atones for sins, and whoever glorifies his mother is like one who lays up treasure. Whoever honors his father will be gladdened by his own children, and when he prays he will be heard. Whoever glorifies his father will have a long life, & whoever obeys the Lord will refresh his mother." Sirach 3:2-6

As noted above, honoring our parents is very rewarding. Of course this all comes naturally from children who were raised in God's design. Unfortunately, truth has become twisted for some, so they may miss the mark and fall short of their responsibilities to express true love. Vices, disorder, self-indulgence, and irresponsibility upset the family balance. Today's new fads of humanism, atheism, and rationalization make the 'human intellect' a false god. They invent truth as they go. No family can survive these lies! Fortunately, after a lot of pain and hurt, sometimes for decades, a glimpse of Light will penetrate this confusion. Genuine truth finally bubbles up when one gets tired of getting a PhD at the "University of Hard Knocks".

Day 241

"God is able to make all grace abound to you, so that always having all sufficiency in everything, you may have an abundance for every good deed." II Corinthians 9:8

Being a Mother is much more than a title of responsibility. A Mother is a woman walking in daily grace.

"His divine power has granted to us everything pertaining to life and godliness, through the true knowledge of Him who called us by His own glory and excellence. For by these He has granted to us His precious and magnificent promises, so that by them you may become partakers of the divine nature, having escaped the corruption that is in the world." II Peter 1:3-4

When temptation comes, say "no" to sin: no way, never, by no means, absolutely not, negative, nix, nay nay!

"I can do all things through Him who strengthens me." Phil. 4:13

Day 242

"The Helper, the Holy Spirit, whom the Father will send
in My name, He will teach you all things." John 14:26

A Prayer to the Holy Spirit - the Secret of Sanctity and Happiness

"I am going to reveal to you the secret of sanctity and happiness.
Every day, for five minutes control your imagination and close your eyes
to all the noises of the world in order to enter into yourself. Then, in the
sanctuary of your baptized soul (which is the temple of the Holy Spirit)
speak to that Divine Spirit, saying to Him:

O Holy Spirit, beloved of my soul, I adore You. Enlighten
me, guide me, strengthen me, console me. Tell me what
I should do; give me Your orders. I promise to submit
myself to all that You desire of me and to accept all
that You permit to happen to me. Let me only know Your Will.

If you do this, your life will flow along happily, serenely, and full of
consolation, even in the midst of trials. Grace will be proportioned
to the trial, giving you the strength to carry it and you will arrive
at the Gate of Paradise, laden with merit. This submission to
the Holy Spirit is the secret of sanctity." Cardinal Mercier

Day 243

"A righteous man who walks in his integrity,
How blessed are his sons after him." Proverbs 20:7

As parents, the most important calling we have is to teach our children
to know, love, and trust God so as to receive the 'crown of righteousness'.
If our children see us trying to live out our faith in love for the
Holy Trinity, then the seed we plant will take root.

**"In the future there is laid up for me the crown of righteousness, which
the Lord, the righteous Judge, will award to me on that day; and
not only to me, but also to all who have loved Him."** II Timothy 4:8

*"One notes first **the poverty or narrowness***
***of man's outlook**, motivated as*
he is by a desire to possess things rather than to relate
them to the truth, and lacking that disinterested,
unselfish, and aesthetic attitude that is born
of wonder in the presence of being and of the beauty which enables one
to see in visible things - the message of the
invisible God who created them.
**In this regard, humanity today must be conscious of its duties and
obligations towards future generations."** Pope Saint John Paul II

Day 244

*"If you give yourself to the hungry and satisfy the desire of the afflicted,
Then your light will rise in darkness and your gloom will become
like midday. And the* LORD *will continually guide you,
And satisfy your desire in scorched places, and give strength
to your bones; and you will be like a watered garden,
And like a spring of water whose waters do not fail." Isaiah 58:10-11*

Motherhood and Fatherhood are 'like a watered garden'.
*Both callings are a beautiful invitation to a way of life where you both
will give of yourself, and will participate in God's tremendous Love
for each one of your Family Members. As your child grows and interacts
with you, you will have many opportunities to see God's generous
outpouring of Grace. Later, you will also experience this sharing of God's
infinite goodness as you see how God works in and through the many lives
your family will touch, along the way. As faithful Christians, we all hope
to grow so that our lives honor Our Lord, but this great love and devotion
should also overflow to bless other lives that God puts on our path.*

Day 245

"You will rejoice in all the good which the LORD your God has given you and your household." Deuteronomy 26:11

From the very beginning, God - the Father, promised us salvation and redemption through His Son, Jesus Christ. A lot of love and preparation went into this sacrifice for each of us. This ultimate sacrificial Love is the foundation and the admirable example we must follow in our life. We too must give our utmost in love for our family, and then celebrate in gratitude the blessings God has so lovingly prepared for our household.

"Blessed be the God and Father of our Lord Jesus Christ, who has blessed us with every spiritual blessing in the heavenly places in Christ, just as He chose us in Him before the foundation of the world, that we would be holy and blameless before Him." Ephesians 1:3-4

God predestined us for glory if we say YES to His holy will. Therefore, look forward with confidence and hope to the fulfillment of His love and power in your family life. Put your trust in the Lord; He always has our best interest at heart. Who could love us more?

Day 246

"For I am confident of this very thing, that He who began a good work in you will perfect it until the day of Christ Jesus." *Philippians 1:6*

Reflect on God's blessings in your life and in the lives of the saints. Their lives are a testimony and a guarantee that grace is at work in us! It is proof that He spurs us on to an ever greater faith, and to an attitude of trustful surrender. Also remember that God's grace always works in the design He has for each of us. Sometimes we feel that we are wandering too long in the desert, but God knows the best way and the best time to perfect His great work in us. His grace is always there; trust His way to perfect your life.

St. Joan of Arc was asked by a tribunal, who hoped to condemn her, if she knew that she was in God's grace, and she replied:
"If I am not, may it please God to put me in it; if I am, may it please God to keep me there."
Acts of the Trial of St. Joan of Arc
"Consider this unique and imposing distinction. Since the writing of human history, Joan of Arc is the only person, of either sex, who has ever held supreme command of the military forces of a nation at the age of seventeen." Louis Kossuth

Day 247

*"If any man would come after me, let him deny himself
and take up his cross and follow me" Matthew 16:24*

As we walk with God, we begin to recognize along the way that we
are growing in understanding and knowledge, and in all honesty,
we recognize that there is a *conversion* taking place in our heart.
This conversion of heart occurs when we become aware of the idols
that do exist in our life. We find ourselves racing about chasing:
The Dream that will make all the Difference. Perhaps it is $$$,
fame, power, vanity, another person, intellect, food, etc., etc., etc.
We've all done it and found the emptiness it all holds. Yet, God
still calls us! He gently steers us to *renew our hearts and
minds,* otherwise we won't find His Truth and true happiness.
*Good news is: that God pursues us. The inspiration of
His Holy Spirit - WOWs us.* We may hear or read a
Holy Scripture that suddenly overwhelms us; yet just
yesterday, it just seemed like Greek to us. Once this happens,
we are never the same. Our thirst and hunger for God's
Word drives us - to know more, love more, and then
to serve. We begin to see that we must *cooperate
with God's grace.* We have
to say **YES to His invitation,** *since He respects our
free will. What a polite and considerate Lord we have,
to show such unconditional and patient love!*

Day 248

"For He said, 'Surely, they are My people,
sons who will not deal falsely.' So He became their Savior.
In all their affliction He was afflicted,
and the angel of His presence saved them;
In His love and in His mercy He redeemed them,
and He lifted them and carried them all the days of old." Isaiah 63:8-9

We are His People – *His presence saved & redeemed us.*
Please note the prophetic tone of Isaiah above, that God's covenant
with His people will be realized through His Son, Jesus.
This Scripture was written hundreds of years before Christ was born.
History then proves God's loyalty. It clearly reveals that God's promises
were kept & are stil kept. We clearly see how devoted He has been to us
through the ages. **"Time" proves God's existence and true love.** *Have*
you noted that all time is based around the life & death of Jesus Christ?
B.C. stands for "Before Christ"(Old Testament) and
A.D. stands for "Anno Domini", which means "in the year of our Lord."
This depicts His life, Death and Resurrection,
(the New Testament). Thus, the
Birth of Jesus Christ - His Incarnation, is the
dividing point of world history.

Ninth Month
(37-40 weeks)

We are on the home stretch now! The miracle of birth is just in sight. You will begin to dilate and efface as your baby drops down lower into position, in preparation for birth. The baby may seem less active, due to his/her increased size and the tight space within your uterus/womb. You may experience some pre-labor contractions called Braxton-Hicks. This is a good sign that your body is getting ready for labor. Generally gestation averages 280 days or 40 weeks. The majority of births take place within 266 to 294 days, or 38 to 42 weeks. At term, the average weight of a baby is six to eight pounds, and most measure between nineteen to twenty one inches. The lanugo and vernix generally disappear by birth. By the end of the month, your baby's heart will be pumping 300 gallons of blood per day! I bet you can't wait to hold your little one, and see his or her beautiful eyes gazing back at you with total love and trust.

Day 249

*"Be strong and courageous, do not be afraid or tremble at them, for the L*ord *your God is the one who goes with you. He will not fail you or forsake you." Deuteronomy 31:6*

*Your ninth month has finally begun! At times your pregnancy may have seemed like a long road, but time will fly now - as you soon approach the day that you **will be holding your precious Gift from God**. It will be incredible to see your baby and hold him or her. Enjoy your child's movement now and don't worry about tomorrow; don't be anxious about the upcoming birth. Pray, call on your Lord – He will be there for you! He will renew your strength and courage. You can count on His faithfulness!*

"God wills that our desire should be exercised in prayer, that we may be able to receive what he is prepared to give." St. Augustine

If you abide in me and I in you, you will bear much fruit; for apart from me you can do nothing." John 15:5

Day 250

"You were tired out by the length of your road,
Yet you did not say, 'It is hopeless.'
You found renewed strength,
Therefore you did not faint." Isaiah 57:10

*Pregnancy can test your endurance and patience, but the reward is so Great! You are blessed as a **Mother with Child** right now; but soon you will be **Blessed with your Child** in your arms! The experience of birth, when you first see your baby is an incredible joy, one that can only be Heaven sent. Soon you will be sharing a whole life together, one with countless blessings! As an extra bonus, you will realize that God has been building you up with many new graces and virtues, so that you can be the mother you need to be for your little one. Fathers are also built up for their important role;yYour Family needs your strength & Godly wisdom!*

"Blessed is a man who perseveres under trial; for once he
has been approved, he will receive the crown of life which the
Lord has promised to those who love Him." James 1:12

Day 251

"For God is not unjust so as to forget your work and the love which you have shown toward His name, in having ministered and in still ministering to the saints." Hebrews 6:10

God will bless you for loving your baby with your whole being.
He knows your heart, the love you have shown, the sacrifices you have made, and all the adjustments you made in your routines & life.
Now you will see even more grace and generosity blessing your path.

"Consider this: whoever sows sparingly will also reap sparingly, and whoever sows bountifully will also reap bountifully."
"Moreover, God is able to make every grace abundant for you, so that in all things, always having all you need, you may have an abundance for every good work."
"You are being enriched in every way for all generosity,
which through us produces thanksgiving to God."
2 Corinthians 9: 6, 8, 11

Day 252

"You have need of endurance, so that when you have done the will of God, you may receive what was promised." Hebrews 10:36

Our Lord suffered greatly in His Passion. He knew what His mission entailed from the beginning. He knew the price for our salvation and for the reparation of our sins. All this Our Lord endured & suffered for us, so that we could receive forgiveness for our sins; and so that we could be adopted children - invited to spend eternal life with the Most Holy Trinity and the Holy Family. God clearly wants us to be part of His Family. In our family, we can also show our children how to walk in a sacrificial love for each other. Then our homes will reflect a joyful and faithful life where God is truly honored.

"Therefore be imitators of God, as beloved children; and walk in love, just as Christ also loved you and gave Himself up for us, an offering and a sacrifice to God as a fragrant aroma." Ephesians 5:1-2

Day 253

"Therefore, since we have so great a cloud of witnesses surrounding us, let us also lay aside every encumbrance and the sin which so easily entangles us, and let us run with endurance the race that is set before us, fixing our eyes on Jesus, the author and perfecter of faith, who for the joy set before Him endured the cross, despising the shame, and has sat down at the right hand of the throne of God." Hebrews 12:1-2

Don't let any anxiety, uneasiness, or faintheartedness overwhelm you. Run your race with the confidence, faith, and love God offers all His children. He wants us all to triumph at the finish line!

"By your endurance you will gain your lives." Luke 21:19

"Consider it all joy, when you encounter various difficulties, knowing that the testing of your faith produces endurance. And let endurance have its perfect result, so that you may be perfect and complete, lacking in nothing." James 1:2-4

Day 254

*"For the eyes of the L*ORD *move to and fro throughout the earth that*
He may strongly support those whose heart is
completely His." II Chronicles 16:9a

If you rely on the Lord, He will amply bless your confidence in Him.
We can only be complete when we decide to join hearts with Our Lord
and work as a Team. This unity will bless you Family Team too!

"Watch over your heart with all diligence,
For from it flows the springs of life.
Put away from you a deceitful mouth and
put devious speech (man's ideologies) far from you.
Let your eyes look directly ahead and
let your gaze be fixed straight in front of you.
Watch the path of your feet
and all your ways will be established.
Do not turn to the right nor to the left;
Turn your foot from evil." Prov. 4:23-27

Day 255

"Look at the birds of the air, that they do not sow, nor reap nor
gather into barns, and yet your heavenly Father feeds them.
Are you not worth much more than they? And who of you by being
worried can add a single hour to his life?" Matthew 6:26-27

Instead of being apprehensive as to how you will care for your baby in
the near future, consider spending the same amount
*of time and energy **Productively – in Prayer.***
Your faith and trust in God will grow as you rest in the
knowledge and peace that God is really in control.

"For this reason I say to you, do not worry about your life,
as to what you will eat; nor for your body, as to what you will put
on. For life is more than food, and the body more than clothing."
"Your Father knows that you need these things.
But seek His kingdom, and these things will be added to you.
Do not be afraid, little flock, for your Father has chosen
gladly to give you the kingdom." Luke 12:22-23, 30-32

Day 256

"Thou art He who brought me forth from the womb;
Thou didst make me trust when upon my mother's breasts." Psalm 22:9

God provides for our needs from the very beginning of life:
from within the womb, upon birth, and in all our developmental
stages. Our baby instinctively trusts these provisions and care.
*As soon as a baby is born, he/she seeks its **"mother's breasts."***
Shouldn't we be as trusting as our baby?

"The Lord is my strength and my shield; my heart trusts in Him,
and I am helped; Therefore my heart exults, and with my song
I shall thank Him." Psalm 28:7

"Trust in the Lord with all your heart and do not lean
on your own understanding." Proverbs 3:5

Day 257

"God's temple in heaven was opened, and the ark of His covenant
could be seen in the temple." "A great sign appeared in the sky, a
woman clothed with the sun, with the moon under her feet, and on
her head a crown of twelve stars. She was with child and wailed
aloud in pain as she labored to give birth." *Revelation 11:19a, 12: 1-2*

Our Lady of Guadalupe said to Juan Diego, "Listen, put it into your heart,
my youngest and dearest son, that the thing that disturbs you, the thing
that afflicts you, is nothing. Do not let your countenance, your heart be
disturbed. Do not fear this sickness of your uncle or any other sickness.
Am I not here, I, who am your Mother?
Are you not under my shadow and protection? Am I not the source of
your joy? Are you not in the hollow of my mantle, in the crossing of
my arms? Do you need anything more? Let nothing else worry you,
or disturb you." Through the *Apparition of Our Lady of Guadalupe,*
millions of indigenous people were converted in Mexico.
"You are the highest honor of our race. Blessed are you, daughter, by
the Most High God, above all the women on earth; and blessed be the
LORD God, the creator of heaven and earth." *Judith 13:18-19; 15:9d*

Day 258

**"The one who does not love does not know God,
For God is love."** *1 John 4:8*

*Every person is called to offer Our Lord a witness of their faith
and love, that no one else can offer for them.*

*"Jesus has revealed to us that 'God is love' and that the highest vocation
of every person is love. In Christ we can find the ultimate reason for
becoming staunch champions of human dignity and courageous builders
of peace. At the same time, each person is called, by grace, to a covenant
with the Creator, called to offer Him a response of faith and love that
no other creature can give in his place. From this supernatural
perspective, one can understand the task entrusted to human beings
to mature in the ability to love and to contribute to the progress of
the world, renewing it in justice and in peace." Pope Benedict XVI*

**"Each of us is the result of a thought of God. Each of us is willed.
Each of us is loved. Each of us is necessary."** *Pope Benedict XVI*

Day 259

**"Have You not made a hedge about him and his house and all that
he has, on every side? You have blessed the work of his hands,
and his possessions have increased in the land."** *Job 1:10*

Pray daily to the Lord to put a **Hedge of Protection** *around you and your
little one, so that your family may be safe from the schemes of the evil one.*

"To have Christian hope means to know about evil and yet
to go to *meet the future with confidence.*
The core of faith rests upon accepting being loved by God,
And therefore to believe is to say Yes, not only to Him,
but to creation, to creatures, and above all, to men;
*To try to see the image of God in each person and
thereby to become a lover.*
That's not easy, but the basic Yes, the conviction
that **God has created men, that He stands behind them**, that
they aren't simply negative, gives love a reference point that enables
it to ground hope on the basis of faith." *Pope Benedict XVI*

Day 260

"For by grace you have been saved through faith;
and that not of yourselves, it is the gift of God." Ephesians 2:8

By grace, Mary gave her consent to be the Mother of Jesus.
In doing so, Mary willed to serve God with her 'YES';
to serve, love, and nurture her Son – the Son of God.
Mary also willingly chose to give her all to God - for our salvation.

"The knot of Eve's disobedience
was untied by Mary's obedience.
The knot which Eve tied through her disbelief,
The Virgin Mary opened by her belief." St Irenaeus of Lyons

"At his hour in the Garden of Gethsemane, Jesus transformed our
rebellious human will into a will conformed and united with the
divine will. *He suffered the whole drama of our autonomy* - and
precisely by placing our will in God's hands, he gives us true freedom:
'Not as I will, but as you will'" (Mt 26: 39). *Pope Benedict XVI*

Day 261

"I waited patiently for the LORD;
And He inclined to me and heard my cry.
He brought me up out of the pit of destruction, out of the miry clay,
And He set my feet upon a rock making my footsteps firm." Ps 40:1-2

At time we all struggle in our faith. We are tested, sometimes to
the point of desolation, where we may feel that all is at a loss.
This inward strife is usually a turning point, where Our Lord is
teaching us how to grow into a deeper and stronger faith.
Climbing from the valley to the mountain top always takes a great effort
on our part – since Our Lord is taking us a step further in trust, faith,
and knowledge. Thank the Lord for His sustaining grace and for
His confidence in you; for He truly knows and believes in you.

"It is not by sidestepping or fleeing from suffering that we are
healed, but rather by our capacity for accepting it, maturing through
it and finding meaning through union with Christ, who suffered
with infinite love." *Pope Benedict XVI, Saved in Hope: Spe Salvi*

Day 262

"Do you not know that you are a temple of God and that the Spirit of God dwells in you?" I Corinthians 3:16

A temple signifies a holy, pure, and consecrated place where one can worship and exalt God. We too are called to be temples or sanctuaries of the Holy Spirit. In being sanctuaries of the Holy Spirit, we are indeed blessed with an incredible honor and responsibility. If we truly comprehend and appreciate the dignity God is bestowing on us with this holy honor, than there should be no doubt as to how much God values each and every one of us. Understanding our worth – in and through God's eyes – should boost our confidence and faith in His great love for each of us. It should also give us a deep respect for the value of every person from the moment of conception until our Father call us home.
God's Spirit makes every life sacred!

"Come Holy Spirit, descend plentifully into my heart. Enlighten the dark corners of this neglected dwelling and scatter there Thy cheerful beams." St. Augustine

Day 263

*"Do not be like them; for your Father knows
what you need before you ask Him." Matthew 6:8*

*Every parent wonders what the state of our world will be like tomorrow,
especially when we see and hear of so much destruction and immorality.
Remember, our children's future lies in God's hands. He will provide
for their care and safety, but He does hope that each of us will become
co-workers with Him in caring for our children's spiritual
and physical upbringing, so they will be properly equipped.
Jesus asks us to be childlike and to trust in His providence.
Your child will teach you how to be childlike again!*

"God is the sovereign master of his plan. But to carry it out he also makes
use of his creatures' co-operation. This use is not a sign of weakness,
but rather a token of almighty God's greatness and goodness. For God
grants his creatures not only their existence, but also the dignity of acting
on their own, of being causes and principles for each other, and thus of
co-operating in the accomplishment of his plan." CCC 306

Day 264

*"Now Abraham and Sarah were old, advanced in age; Sarah was past
childbearing. And the L*ORD *said to Abraham, "Why did Sarah laugh,
saying, 'Shall I indeed bear a child, when I am so old?' Is anything
too difficult for the L*ORD*? At the appointed time I will return to you, at
this time next year, and Sarah will have a son." Genesis 18:11, 13-14*

*Since God is the Author of all life, how can we then - who were created
by God - question His ability or intent? His wisdom, power, and glory
are above all human knowledge and understanding. God has given us so
many wonderful examples in Scripture - that prove again and again - His
loving faithfulness to us. His Word is evidence that He can and will deliver
what He promises. These gifts were not just for the past – they continue to
bless our present time – for God is alive and dwells with us. Go to the
Blessed Sacrament to adore Him, and see how He will bless you.
"This is My Body" (cf. Luke 22:19-20).*

**"It is God who is at work in you, both to will and to work for
His good pleasure."** *Philippians 2:13*

Day 265

"I have set the LORD continually before me;
Because He is at my right hand, I will not be shaken.
Therefore my heart is glad and my glory rejoices;
My flesh also will dwell securely." Psalms 16:8-9

Your baby's upcoming birth is probably ever present on your mind. As women, we know that we will labor to bring our baby into this world; but as mothers we worry even more about our baby's health, that all may go well for our little one. 'Set the Lord continually before you', and you will rest securely that all will go well on your *Baby's Birthday.*

"Now it shall be, if you diligently obey the LORD your God, being careful to do all His commandments which I command you today, the LORD your God will set you high above all the nations of the earth. All these blessings will come upon you and overtake you if you obey the LORD your God: "Blessed shall you be in the city, and blessed shall you be in the country. ***"Blessed shall be the offspring of your body." Deuteronomy 28:1-4a***

Day 266

"Can you discover the depths of God?
Can you discover the limits of the Almighty?" Job 11:7

We are so blessed to have been created by such a noble God. God's dignity and grandeur are beyond all comprehension or measure. Above all, we are blessed to be His children. God's great love for us has no limitations. Throughout Scriptures and the lives of the saints, God is uniquely and absolutely HOLY. He is so unique and so perfect that His existence cannot be compared to any other existence. All began in & with Him! God is incomparable, boundless, and Supreme Above All.

"What He is, by *essence and nature*, is altogether beyond our comprehension and knowledge," *St. John of Damascus*

"Through Him all things were made; without Him nothing was made that has been made." John 1:3

Day 267

"If you would direct your heart right
and spread out your hand to Him,
Your life would be brighter than noonday;
Darkness would be like the morning.
Then you would trust, because there is hope;
And you would look around and rest securely." Job 11:13, 17-18

Take the time to reread the story of Job. For someone who suffered so much, you would never expect to find such great faith, nor such reliance upon God. No matter what happened, Job was steadfast in his faith. He always directed his heart towards his heavenly Father, and God rewarded the efforts of his devoted heart.

"Create in me a clean heart, O God, and renew a
steadfast spirit within me." Psalm 51:10

"Therefore, my beloved brethren, be steadfast, immovable, always abounding in the work of the Lord, knowing that your toil is not in vain in the Lord." 1 Corinthians 15:58

Day 268

"Why are you in despair, O my soul?
And why have you become disturbed within me?
Hope in God, for I shall yet praise Him,
The help of my countenance and my God." Psalms 42:11

There are times when we feel that life can really deplete & overwhelm
us. You may be particularly vulnerable right now, as you await a
momentous step in life. Don't get disturbed by all the upcoming
changes. Yes, the birth of your child will alter your life. There will
be adjustments, but it will all be positive growth. Remember that
God, in all His wisdom, is giving you the gift of motherhood! He
will renew your spirit. God is also giving you a precious life to
care for. God believes in you! He will equip and direct you.
God has wonderful plans for you and for your baby. This adorable
life will give and share all your love. You have a lot of love and
life to look forward to; a lot of love to give & to receive!
"Yet those who wait for the Lord Will gain new strength; they will
mount up with wings like eagles, they will run and not get tired, they
will walk and not become weary." Isaiah 40:31

Day 269

"So that you will not be sluggish, be imitators of those who through faith and patience inherit the promises. For when God made the promise to Abraham, since He could swear by no one greater, He swore by Himself, saying, "I WILL SURELY BLESS YOU AND I WILL SURELY MULTIPLY YOU." *And so, having patiently waited, he obtained the promise."* Hebrews 6:12-15

God kept His promise to Abraham - though Abraham had to wait decades before he was blessed with Isaac. It was his son, Isaac, who carried the faith and God's promises to future generations. We need to learn how to trust God's design for our life, and for our children's. God's plans are not based on our time schedule. So be at peace that God always wills what is best for us. Remember, God has also blessed you with a life that is so unique & miraculous, that there has never been another person like your little one.

"May the Lord lift up His countenance on you, And give you peace." Numbers 6:26

Day 270

*"By this all men will know that you are My disciples,
if you have love for one another." John 13:35*

*"A hundred years from now
It will not matter
What my bank account was,
What kind of house I lived in,
What kind of car I drove,
Nor the clothes I wore...
BUT
The world may be a little better
Because, I was important
In the life of a child."*
Anonymous

"At the end of our life, we shall all be judged by charity."
St. John of the Cross

Day 271

"For whatever was written in earlier times was written for our instruction, so that through perseverance and the encouragement of the Scriptures we might have hope." Romans 15:4

Through Scripture we find the meaning of life.
Our existence, dignity, and worth are all found in God's Word.
Scripture witnesses God's great love for us - in & through His actions.
Really ponder this ultimate gift of love, that
Our Father freely offered us His
ONLY Son, Jesus. Could you offer your only child? Yes, this was
God's design, that in Jesus, God's word became flesh, and His
merciful covenant with His people was realized. And through
Christ's great love and sacrifice, our sins are forgiven, so that
we can be given the gift of hope – an everlasting life with Our
Lord. It is very important that we teach our children this Truth,
so that their lives may have hope, purpose, and direction.
"As a mother delights in taking her child on her knees, in caressing and
feeding him, so does our God delight in treating with
love and tenderness those souls who give themselves
entirely to Him, and place all their hopes
in His goodness and bounty." *St Alphonsus Liguori, Doctor of the Church*

Day 272

"The LORD is the one who goes ahead of you; He will be with you. He will not fail you or forsake you. Do not fear or be dismayed." Deuteronomy 31:8

This Scripture gave me so much peace with my first childbirth. It was close to Christmas time, so I pondered Christ's birth. When it was time for Jesus to be born, His parents had to travel to Bethlehem. Joseph sought shelter, but there was no room at the inns. They ended up in a stable for animals. Today it is hard for a woman to contemplate giving birth in a stable, especially since we have become accustomed to the idea of sterilized hospitals. Yet every year we celebrate Christ's birth with beautiful manger scenes at church, in our homes, and at Christmas plays. Mary & Joseph are always smiling peacefully. The angels are singing joyfully. The shepherds and kings are worshipping reverently. It's a holy night, and the heavens are lit up with the brightest star ever recorded. No one worried that the stable and conditions were far from being pristine. All eyes and hearts were on the fact that God had decorated the heavens, and had sent shepherds and kings ahead to adore the King of kings. All was perfect!

Day 273

"Thy kingdom come. Thy will be done,
On earth as it is in heaven." Matthew 6:10

What is God's Perspective? To follow His will!
If we keep a pure heart and then choose to follow God's holy will,
we will see more clearly to understand His truth. Our Lord came for
this purpose: to save us & to teach us to be true children of God;
and to proclaim His kingdom – that we may live His ways "on earth
as it is in heaven." Then our focus and understanding of life will
*reflect God's desire for our life. So **be** what God always intended*
you to be from all eternity. Follow His loving plan just for you. Pray
and ask Our Lord to help you see life from His point of view.

"For this reason I bow my knees before the Father, from whom
every family in heaven and on earth derives its name, that He would
grant you, according to the riches of His glory, to be strengthened
with power through His Spirit in your inner being, so that Christ
may dwell in your hearts through faith; and that you, being
rooted and grounded in love, may be able to comprehend with all
the saints what is the breadth and length and height and depth,
and to know the love of Christ which surpasses knowledge,
that you may be filled up to all the fullness of God." Ephesians 3:14-19

Day 274

"I will put My law within them and on their heart I will write it; and I will be their God, and they shall be My people." Jeremiah 31:33

*As God's people, He has infused natural law into our hearts. This law reflects His Divine Law. Yet God has also given us a free will – to test our hearts true loyalty. So be careful to guard your heart, mind, and will. **It is in our heart that we decide for or against God.** Remember, the two main principles of your soul are your mind and will, which are influenced by your heart. From this frame of reference, you will be making decisions and directing yourself - and your family. If our free will seeks God's perfect will and love – we will be happy. We are His people! We were designed from the beginning to seek our destiny: eternal life with God.*

"For where your treasure is, there will your heart be also." Mt 6:21

"In the newborn child is realized the common good of the family."
Pope Saint John Paul II, Letters to Families

Day 275

"Train up a child in the way he should go,
Even when he is old he will not depart from it." Proverbs 22:6

"Our children depend on us for everything: their health,
their nutrition, their security, and their coming to know and
love God. For all of this, they look to us with trust, hope,
and expectation. Love of the child - is where love
and peace must begin. Pray together, for we must bring
the presence of God into the family."
Mother Teresa of Calcutta

The *witness and example* parents give is the most important aspect of their child's upbringing. Parents exert the most meaningful direction in their child's moral training. In truth, our words to our child are meaningless unless our own actions confirm them. You may be telling your child to say their morning and evening prayers, but if you don't say them as a family, then the words will be void and empty. A Family's greatest responsibility is to direct the *fullness of life* back to God, Our Creator.
Your words will tell others what you think.
Your actions will tell others what you believe.

Day 276

"The wisdom from above is first pure, then peaceable, gentle,
reasonable, full of mercy and good fruits, unwavering,
without hypocrisy. And the seed whose fruit is righteousness
is sown in peace by those who make peace." James 3:17-18
"We are moving toward a dictatorship of relativism which
does not recognize anything as certain, and which has as its
highest goal one's own ego and one's own desires." Relativism
attacks our capacity to seek and know the truth, including
the moral truth. A dictatorship of relativism imposes
by real cultural force (and by political force) *a no-standard standard.*
Cardinal Ratzinger said in his *Without Roots*, "The more
relativism becomes the generally accepted way of thinking, the
more it *tends toward intolerance. Political correctness ... seeks*
to establish the domain of a single way of thinking and speaking.
It is vital that we oppose this imposition of a
new pseudo-enlightenment, which threatens freedom of thought
as well as freedom of religion." *Benjamin Wiker, Ph.D.*
May the Holy Spirit bless your Family with
His wisdom, that you may dwell
and grow in God's pure love, peace and truth. For without God's design,
we will wander from God's standard and moral law.

Day 277

"Love...rejoices with the truth; bears all things, believes all things, hopes all things, endures all things." 1 Corinthians 13:6b-7

Love is Demanding

"The love which the Apostle Paul celebrates in the First Letter to the Corinthians - the love which is "patient and kind", and "endures all things" (1 Cor. 13:4, 7) - is certainly a demanding love. But this is precisely the **source of its beauty***: by the very fact that it is demanding, it builds up the true good of man and allows it to radiate to others. The good, says Saint Thomas, is by its nature "diffusive". Love is true when it creates the good of persons and of communities; it creates that good and gives it to others. Only the one who is able to be demanding with himself in the name of love can also demand love from others. Love is demanding. It makes demands in all human situations; it is even more demanding in the case of those who are open to the Gospel. People need to rediscover this demanding love, for it is the truly the firm* **foundation of the family***, a foundation able to 'endure all things'."*

Pope Saint John Paul II, Letter to Families

Day 278

*"God has made everything appropriate in its time. I
know that there is nothing better - than to rejoice and to
do good in one's lifetime; moreover, that every man ...
sees good in all his labor - it is the gift of God."*
Ecclesiastes 3:11, 12-13

*I am very grateful for God's providence, for all the love & sacrifices
made through the generations that blessed my life - because I know:
I am the product of the Holy Trinity's loving sacrifices for me;
I am the product of my Grandparents' &
Parents' labor & sacrifices for me;
I am the product of many Teachers: Religious
& Family that sacrifice for me;
I am the product of my Husband's & my Friends' sacrifices for me.*

**"We should not accept in silence the benefactions of God,
but return thanks for them." St Basil** – *Be Grateful!*

*"I think the world today is upside down. Everybody seems to be in such
a terrible rush, anxious for greater development and greater riches
and so on. There is much suffering because there is so very little love
in homes and in family life. We have no time for our children, we have
no time for each other; there is no time to enjoy each other. In the
home begins the disruption of the peace of the world." **Mother Teresa**
- Please take time; there is an appropriate time for everything!*

Day 279

"Worthy are You, our Lord and our God, to receive glory and honor and power; for You created all things, and because of Your will they existed, and were created." Revelation 4:11

God has called you to Motherhood & your spouse to Fatherhood.
You have both cooperated with God in bringing this new life into being. Though both of you are making adjustments at home and possibly at work, it is the Mother with Child that has adjusted the most as her body changes to carry a life, and now to give birth. Miraculously, the woman's body "knows" what to do, since God has written this mysterious "code" into a woman's design. It is God that guides these wonderful changes & growth.

"Whenever a woman is in labor she has pain, because her hour has come; but when she gives birth to the child, she no longer remembers the anguish because of the joy that a child has been born into the world." *John 16:21*

It is God that will guide you and your little one as you labor & give birth. Trust Him, He's in control and He knows what He is doing!

Day 280

"This is the day which the Lord has made;
Let us rejoice and be glad in it." Psalm 118:24

I pray that the Lord will pour out His blessings and graces on you and
your baby during delivery. May the Lord also bless the doctors
and nurses caring for both of you. May you, your spouse, and
your family continue to grow in God's love and wisdom;
that you may all abound with the Gifts of the Holy Spirit.
Oh, the incredible JOY when you first gaze into your child's eyes;
what wonder & awe at the first touch & embrace of your offspring!
How can we ever thank God enough for His wonderful Gift of Life!

"Behold, children are a gift of the Lord, The fruit of the womb
is a reward." Psalm 127:3

"I pray that the eyes of your heart may be enlightened in order
that you may know the hope to which He has called you, the riches
of His glorious inheritance in His holy people." Ephesians 1:18
God bless your Family!

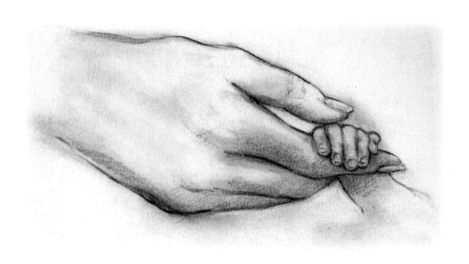

Dedicate your Baby to the Lord

"I prayed for this child, and the LORD granted my request.
Now I, in turn, give him to the LORD;
as long as he lives, he shall be dedicated to the LORD." I Samuel 1:27-28

"Jesus said, 'Permit the children to come to Me, and do not hinder
them, for the kingdom of God belongs to such as these.'" *Luke 18:16*

Family Honor & Authority

"God sets a father in honor over his children;
a mother's authority he confirms over her sons.
Whoever honors his father atones for sins, and preserves
himself from them. When he prays, he is heard;
he stores up riches who reveres his mother.
Whoever honors his father is gladdened by children,
and, when he prays, is heard.
Whoever reveres his father will live a long life; and
he who obeys his father brings comfort to his mother." Sirach 3:2-6

More Blessings to Come!

I wrote this book to inspire Parents, especially Mothers, during their time
of gestation - an important time of development and spiritual formation.
Nonetheless, I recently, felt prompted to write an encouraging note to
the Youth, especially after seeing their brave witness
to faith as they courageously proclaim God's Truth.
What incredible Cheerleaders for Life!

Dear brothers and sisters, giving thanks to God for you
is not only the right thing to do, but it is our duty to God
because of the really wonderful way your faith has grown
and because of your growing love for each other."
2 Thessalonians 1:3

Our Cheerleaders for Life - the Millennials,
will persevere with their holy zeal for the Culture of Life!
They are the 'New Springtime' that is promoting
fervor & fire in our souls.

*They have witnessed to truth, since many of them carry the battle scars
left behind from all the confusion previous generations handed them.*

*This Generation knows and understands the value and worth of marriage,
faithfulness, chastity, and raising a family that follows God's design.*

*The rejection of God in humanism and the lies of relativism – are
false cultural ideologies that have failed. Truth always surfaces!
Marriage, Family and Life are worth it; we can grow in virtues
to Build each other UP! We aren't weak, useless, negative beings or
commodities to be used and then tossed away! God created us
in goodness with a body & soul made in His Image!
This Generation will make a difference because
they have Hope in their Hearts, and they revere God!*

"The Spirit of truth… will guide you." *John 16:13a*

**"Thus says the LORD, even the captives of the mighty man
will be taken away, and the prey of the tyrant will be rescued;
For I will contend with the one who contends with you,
and I will save your sons."** *Isaiah 49:25*

*Your generation won't compromise on the Truth;
Your generation will overturn Roe v. Wade.*

"How could any die, who had not previously lived?"
De Anima 25, Tertullian (c. 160 – 240 A.D.)

So prepare & put on the **Armor of God** *and carry the*
Sword of Truth*! Witness to LIFE with the spirit of zeal God gave you:*

**"Watch over your heart with all diligence,
For from it flows the springs of life.
Put away from you a deceitful mouth and
put devious speech (man's ideologies) far from you.
Let your eyes look directly ahead and
let your gaze be fixed straight in front of you.
Watch the path of your feet
and all your ways will be established.
Do not turn to the right nor to the left;
Turn your foot from evil."** *Proverbs 4:23-27*

"Listen, put it into your heart,... that the thing
that afflicts you, is nothing.
Do not let your countenance, your heart be disturbed.
Am I not here, I, who am your Mother?
Are you not under my shadow and protection?"
Our Lady of Guadalupe

"Let no one look down on the youth. Be their ideal; let them follow
the way you teach and live; be an example in speech, conduct, love,
faith and purity, for those who believe." *1Timothy 4:12*

"Now may the God of hope fill you with all joy and peace
in believing, so that you will abound in hope by
the power of the Holy Spirit." *Romans 15:13*

"When you live in holiness,
when you really try to stop sinning,
you become braver.
You become more courageous,
you become a man of your word.
You become a man of conviction
that you're not willing to sell out and
you're really a true knight in shining armor."
Jim Caviezel, Actor

*"A producer asked **Kathy Ireland** if she was pro-choice.*
Even as she answered "yes," she knew she wasn't.
"I didn't want to be pro-life then," she said. However, after looking
through her husband's medical textbooks she found scientific proof
that the embryo is a human being, "What I read was astounding
and I learned that at the moment of conception a new life comes
into being. The complete genetic blueprint is there, the DNA is
determined, the blood type is determined, the sex is determined, the
unique set of fingerprints that nobody has had or ever will have is
already there." She then called an abortion clinic and asked for
their "best argument" for abortion, and was told two things:
that it was a clump of cells, and that "if we get it early enough, it
doesn't even look like a baby." Even a supermodel knew
that all human beings are, technically speaking, "clumps of cells,"
and that "just like a baby doesn't look like a teenager,
and a teenager doesn't look like a senior citizen, it's
what humans look like at that stage of development.*
It's just that we're not used to seeing it."
At a social function she remarked that "every child is wanted"...
*and that **"God doesn't make mistakes."***
She also warned against turning abortion into a "political football,"
and said that while Roe v. Wade must be overturned,
"what we need to do is change hearts".
"Don't let anyone silence you, and please don't let your
own fear silence you," Kathy Ireland.

Live Action blog, Kristen Walker, 11/11/11

About the Author

Annette Marian is a Roman Catholic wife & mother, scientist & teacher, and a Pro-Life advocate who has worked with the youth and the Culture of Life to direct souls towards the Holy Trinity's great love and mercy. She feels called to be of service to others in thanksgiving for the incredible love and noble grace God always showers on all of us, as His beloved children.

"Glorify God in your body!" 1 Cor. 6:20

Printed in the United States
By Bookmasters